THE ADVANCED
HOW TO
BECOME MONEY
WORKBOOK

by Gary M. Douglas

It doesn't matter whether you've got a million dollars or fifty cents. The issues of money are tough for everyone.

~ *Gary Douglas*

The original *How to Become Money Workbook* was first published in the early 1990s. Tens of thousands of people from around the world have used this book to create greater ease and clarity with money and to have more in their life.

The Advanced How to Become Money Workbook picks up where the original leaves off and offers more advanced questions and processes about how to become money and what that can mean for you.

Please do all the questions in the first *How to Become Money Workbook* before you begin to work with the questions in this workbook.

HOW TO USE
THIS WORKBOOK

The source of all change and all possibility is becoming aware of the limitations you have chosen. When you truly become aware of what a limitation is, you will tend to no longer buy it as true. That's the direction we're heading—getting free from your limitations about money.

This workbook is full of questions and processes designed to get you to look at your limitations about money again, and again, and again—until you finally realize, "Wait a minute! This is a stupid point of view. I would choose this for what reason?"

There doesn't have to be a limitation unless you choose it.

It's Not About Logic

A lady who was working with these questions told me she was having a tough time getting more than three or four answers to some of the questions in this workbook. She said that some questions didn't even make sense to her and she would zone out when she asked them.

Here's something you need to know about these questions: When you try to find the sense in them, it means that you are trying to find the logic according to this reality. This has nothing to do with what is actually so.

Someone else told me she got similar answers no matter what the question was. I said, "You're trying to look from the point of view of logic, aren't you?

She said, "Yes, a little bit."

I asked, "Is money ever really logical? No, money is just energy. You keep trying to look for the logic of what is real and true instead of the awareness of you, which is the only source of what is real and true."

You are the only source of what is real and true for you, but you keep trying to look to your sense of what's logical, or you try to look to this reality, or to that which you can define and confine, or to that which somebody else will validate. What if everything that is true for you is far beyond what anybody else can see? Looking at that is the only way you can create your financial reality.

If you're trying to take your monetary reality to a different level, you are going to come up against questions you don't think are working. Keep asking them and writing down your answers, because the idea is to change your reality about money.

Work These Questions Over Several Times

A guy who took the Advanced How to Become Money class with me said that he had listened to the classes more than five times and that he heard different things each time he listened. He asked, "Is it that I forget what I heard or what I learned? What is it?"

I said, "As you clear off different layers of limitation, you hear things from a different place."

The guy said, "Yes. That's what I am seeing. Different things come up, different things appear that I wouldn't have recognized before."

That's the reason you need to repeat the exercises and questions in this workbook. When you do them, you start opening the door to creating from a different place—and a different possibility begins to occur. This is the way things work. You've had billions of years of creating your life as misery. So you might need to work these questions over several times.

If you have only two or three answers to a particular question at a particular time, that may be the most you can get in any one day. Why would that be? Because you have never looked for infinite possibility with money. You have only looked at the possibilities of money based on this reality, so you won't have answers for those questions.

If you really want to get clarity about money, you need to do these questions again and again. If you do them once in the morning and again later in the day, you are going to find you have two or three more answers. Are those going to be all the answers you can get? For that day, yes. Then you can do them again the next day or later in the week.

~ Gary Douglas

TABLE OF CONTENTS

Chapter One: **Being and Receiving** 9

Chapter Two: **What If Everything Was About Possibility and Nothing Was About the Problem?** 25

Chapter Three: **Trusting Yourself** 40

Chapter Four: **Sex, Money, and Receiving** 53

Chapter Five: **What Do You Want to Do with Your Life?** 69

Chapter Six: **Wealth and Fortune** 82

Chapter Seven: **Enthusiasm for Living** 94

Chapter Eight: **Money Is Easy** 104

Chapter Nine: **A Future Beyond Anything You Have Ever Seen** 119

CHAPTER ONE

BEING AND RECEIVING

Here is your first question. Please write down ten answers.

QUESTION ONE: *What am I refusing to be that if I would be it would create too much money in my life?*

_____

_____

_____

_____

_____

One of the key elements to having an enormous, amazing, and creative life is the willingness to receive, because in order to receive, you have to be willing to be. What you are not willing to be is that which keeps you from receiving.

True receiving is being able to receive all the information there is. It's the capacity to perceive everything without a point of view. You have to be willing to receive if you are going to have the life you truly desire.

A participant in the Advanced How to Become Money class said, "As I asked the question 'What are you refusing to be that if you would be it would create too much money in your life?' I became aware of things I was refusing that were actually possible. What would it take to choose more of those?"

If you are willing to be all money, you can have all money. If you are willing to be all control, you can have all control. If you are willing to be totally different, you can have totally different.

> What have you made so vital and valuable about your definitions of receiving that keep you from actually being that which can receive? Everything

that is times a godzillion, will you destroy and uncreate it all? Right and Wrong, Good and Bad, POD and POC, All 9, Shorts, Boys, and Beyonds.®[1]

Whenever you define something, you limit what it can be and what you can receive. That's because definition, by definition alone, is limitation. What have you made so vital and valuable about your definitions of receiving that keep you from actually being that which you can receive?

> What are you refusing to be that you truly could be, that if you would actually be it would allow you to receive everything you have decided you cannot have, you cannot be, you cannot do, you cannot create, you cannot generate? Everything that is times a godzillion, will you destroy and uncreate it all? Right and Wrong, Good and Bad, POD and POC, All 9, Shorts, Boys, and Beyonds.

A class participant who was working with this question said, "I seem to create value systems about what I would or wouldn't do to get money. When I ask the question about what I'm refusing to be, something comes up about being a grifter."

A grifter is a con artist or a hustler, someone who lies or cons people into giving them money. I said, "Everything you have done to not be a grifter is what keeps you being a grifter trying not to be a grifter to prove you are not a grifter so you can grift people without grifting them. You've already decided that you are grifter in order not to go there. You have to ask: 'What am I refusing to be that if I would be it would create too much money in my life?'

"You have to ask that because you have a lot of points of view about this that you don't even know you have. Being a grifter or a con artist is probably one of ten thousand points of view you have. You are trying not to be everything you could be that would create too much money in your life in order to justify that it is okay to have not enough. You don't ask: 'What would it be like if I had $100 million a year for all eternity?'"

That's your second question.

---

1. "Right and Wrong, Good and Bad, POD and POC, All 9, Shorts, Boys, and Beyonds" is the Access Consciousness Clearing Statement®. You can read more about it at the end of this book. For more information about what the words mean and how it works, visit: http://www.accessconsciousness.com/content60.asp

QUESTION TWO: *What would it be like if I had $100 million a year for all eternity?*

_____

_____

_____

_____

_____

Most of us feel like grifters or con artists or frauds because we don't trust that we know what we know when we know that we know it. We doubt ourselves. How much doubt are you using to stop the money? How much doubt are you using to create the lack of money you are choosing?

QUESTION THREE: *How much doubt am I using to create the lack of money I am choosing?*

_____

_____

_____

_____

_____

Are you willing to be the voice of all possibility? What would it be like if you had $100 million a year for all eternity? It's an energy. It's not about what you can buy, it's about what you can be.

You decide you are not willing to be something because you think it is wrong. For example, I recently had to teach Dain how to lie. His point of view was "You have to be honest. You have to tell the truth, the whole truth, and nothing but the truth, so help you God!" This meant anybody could lie to him, and would, and did.

You have to be willing to be and do anything to create a greater possibility. The only reason you don't have huge amounts of money is because you are not willing to be or do whatever it takes to create a greater possibility.

If you say, "I don't want to be that person," is that a judgment? Is that a conclusion? Is that a definition of you? Yes. Wherever you define any part of you, that becomes the place you can't be all of you.

How many definitions are you using to avoid the money you could be choosing? Everything that is times a godzillion, will you destroy and uncreate it all? Right and Wrong, Good and Bad, POD and POC, All 9, Shorts, Boys, and Beyonds.

If you want to become money, you have to be willing to be what creates money instead of being that which makes you wrong.

Let's say you are interested in playing with jewelry as a way of making money. What would you have to be to make it so joyful for people to buy from you that they would find it happening with ease? Rather than trying to convince people they should buy something, what if you be that which will allow them to buy it? This, by the way, applies to every Access facilitator on the planet.

Humanoids and Money

You have to be willing to see what will create for you, not what you *think* is going to create for you. Most business plans are based on a human reality, but you are a humanoid[2], and humanoids create from a different possibility and a different reality.

As a humanoid, you are more interested in what you can create than the money you get from the creation. You do things not because of the money but because of what might be created. You create something, and if somebody sees how great it is, you give it to them rather than being aware of what it is going to create. That's the way humanoids are. They are idiots and I love them! That's the way I am, and I do it a lot.

We think that people will receive something if we do it for free, but generally speaking, people do not receive that which is free. The more expensive it is, the more valuable it is to them. That is this reality. That is why diamonds are considered more valuable than zircon. Both of them shine, both of them come out of the dirt, both of them need to be

---

2. There are two species of two-legged beings on this planet. We call them humans and humanoids. They look alike, they walk alike, they talk alike, and they often eat alike, but the reality is they're different. Humans will always tell you how you're wrong, how they're right, and how you shouldn't change anything. They say things like, "We don't do things like that, so don't even bother." They are the ones who ask, "Why are you changing that? It's fine the way it is."
Humanoids take a different approach. They are always looking at things and asking, "How can we change that? What will make that better? How can we outdo this?" They're the people who have created all the great art, the great literature, and the great progress on the planet.

manipulated to look prettier, but one is worth huge amounts of money and the other is worth basically nothing.

QUESTION FOUR: *What would I have to charge in order for people to receive what I have to give?*

_____

_____

_____

_____

Everything that doesn't allow that times a godzillion, will you destroy and uncreate it all? Right and Wrong, Good and Bad, POD and POC, All 9, Shorts, Boys, and Beyonds.

QUESTION FIVE: *Where have I refused to be the real source of change that eliminates the awareness of the limitation I have chosen?*

_____

_____

_____

_____

What have you made so vital and valuable about your definitions of receiving that keep you from actually being that which can receive? Everything that is times a godzillion, will you destroy and uncreate it all? Right and Wrong, Good and Bad, POD and POC, All 9, Shorts, Boys, and Beyonds.

What are you refusing to be that you truly could be that if you would actually be it would allow you to have everything you would like to have and cannot be, do, have, create, and generate? Everything that is times a godzillion, will you destroy and uncreate it all? Right and Wrong, Good and Bad, POD and POC, All 9, Shorts, Boys, and Beyonds.

Most people are not willing to have a life that is easy. They're not willing to demand and receive in their world the level of ease that will create their life.

An Access facilitator told me, "When I create a class, sometimes I have the point of view that I have to receive a certain amount of money for it to be created. When I destroy and uncreate that point of view and I have fun and experience the joy of creating classes, it is like the universe gifts me money and wealth."

I asked, "Do you know what the most important thing you just said is? You said the one thing that will make everything work for you and you ignored it: 'When I have no point of view and I create classes for the fun and joy of creating, the universe gifts me money and wealth.' The reality is money only comes to the parties where there is consciousness and fun."

QUESTION SIX: *What have I made so appropriate about money that I can't have the fun and joy of money?*

_____

_____

_____

_____

Most people think the fun and joy of money is getting drunk and disorderly. That's not the fun and joy of money. The fun and joy of money is the ability to change people's reality with money. What have you made the definition of money that keeps you from having it, enjoying it, and creating beyond this reality?

QUESTION SEVEN: *What have I made the definition of money that keeps me from having it, enjoying it, and creating beyond this reality?*

_____

_____

_____

_____

QUESTION EIGHT: *What am I trying to create in order to prove I don't have to have too much money?*

_____

_____

_____

_____

_____

If you ask that question twenty or thirty times, you will become aware of what you are doing to avoid money instead of having it.

> What are you trying to create in order to prove you don't have too much money? Everything that is times a godzillion, will you destroy and uncreate it all? Right and Wrong, Good and Bad, POD and POC, All 9, Shorts, Boys, and Beyonds.

You want to have just enough—but not too much—because if you have just enough you can get most of what you want so you don't have to deprive yourself totally, but depriving yourself totally actually sounds like a good idea to you in the long run.

> What are you trying to create in order to prove you don't have too much money? Everything that is times a godzillion, will you destroy and uncreate it all? Right and Wrong, Good and Bad, POD and POC, All 9, Shorts, Boys, and Beyonds.

Instead of having just enough, what if you created something that was beyond this reality? Creating beyond this reality is not trying to define you or anything you do based on anybody else's point of view. It's a necessity if you want to change this reality.

> Everything that doesn't allow you to be that, will you destroy and uncreate it all? Right and Wrong, Good and Bad, POD and POC, All 9, Shorts, Boys, and Beyonds.

QUESTION NINE: *What have I defined money as that it actually isn't?*

_____

_____

_____

_____

_____

Until you know what you define money as, you can't undo that which is a limitation of what you receive. Your definition of money becomes a limitation of what you can receive. It also becomes what you've decided you cannot have. In order to have something, you have to be willing to be it. If you're not willing to be it, you can't have it, and if you're not willing to have it, you can't be it.

Being Money

Being money is never seeing it as separate from you. It's seeing money as something that loves you better than your parents do. Money doesn't do anything. It simply increases your capacity to have a different choice.

QUESTION TEN: *What's the greatest amount of money I can willingly be?*

_____

_____

_____

_____

_____

Did you read that question and say, "Huh?" If you are not willing to be a $100 million dollars, you can only create one million dollars. Whatever you have had as your annual income is the greatest amount of money you are willing to be. Your annual income defines the greatest amount of money you are willing to be.

How do you change that? You look at it and you ask: "What have I defined as the maximum amount of money I am willing to be?" Whatever amount you come up with, question it. Ask: "Is that really enough for me?"

"What's the largest amount of money I am willing to be?" is an important question. Here's why: If you look at your life and say, "The greatest amount of money I am willing to be is $50,000 or $100,000," is that going to create what you want to create? No. Is that going to give you the choice that creates a greater possibility in the world? No.

If you ask for the greatest amount you are willing to be, then you have to be willing to be that much money. Are you not willing to be a multimillionaire?

What is the greatest amount of money you are willing to be? Everything that brought up times a godzillion, will you destroy and uncreate it all? Right and Wrong, Good and Bad, POD and POC, All 9, Shorts, Boys, and Beyonds.

The Capacity to Be

The amount of money you are willing to be determines the amount of change you can create in the world. Many people want to change the world, but they are not willing to be the amount of money it takes to change the world. How is that going to work?

We are starting to develop a resort and education center in Costa Rica where people come to learn to live with the elegance of the Earth and not abuse it. Did I know how I was going to pay for it? No. Did I know where the money was going to come from? No. Did I know that somehow I could get it? Absolutely.

Why did I know I could get it? Because I know the universe desires to support what I am trying to create. This allows the universe a different possibility, and I am willing to be whatever it takes, no matter what that looks like, to create a different possibility in the world. Are you? If my being that required that I had to die in order to pay for our center in Costa Rica, I would do that. This is a whole different way of looking at the world. When I am willing to be whatever it takes to create a different possibility, the universe will make sure that the money can show up in my life.

Recognize that when you are doing that which supports the consciousness of the world, the consciousness of the world supports you. Does the consciousness of the world desire you to have a BMW? No, it doesn't. But if you support the world with everything you do, and you request a BMW, you'll get a BMW.

Money Is Not a Source of Creation

A lot of people think of money as a tool for creating, but money is not a source of creation. *You* are the source of creation that creates money. Money is a lazy pile of shit. It doesn't want to work that hard. You, on the other hand, are not a lazy pile of shit. You like to work hard because it makes you happy.

Are creation and creativity a source of money? No. Money is a by-product of what you create. When you eat, do you automatically create shit? No. Shit is a by-product of eating. That's an obnoxious way of putting it. It's about how you facilitate money and how you facilitate change in the world with money.

QUESTION ELEVEN: *What can I do or choose that will create greater possibility in the world right away?*

_____

_____

_____

_____

Possibility does not come from money. It is about what you can choose and what you can do because of choices that create greater possibility.

QUESTION TWELVE: *What can I be that I am not being that if I would be it would exponentialize my receiving off the charts of this reality?*

_____

_____

_____

_____

Receiving can only occur by what you are willing to be. You have to be a whole lot more than you think you can actually be to increase your capacity to receive.

I have looked at thousands of things with respect to how they might be, how they should be, how they could be, or how they ought to be. Was any of it true? No. Did any of it mean anything? No.

QUESTION THIRTEEN: *What have I chosen as the sum of what I can be, do, have, create, and generate that keeps me living in this reality rather than having my reality?*

_____

_____

_____

_____

_____

Paying Whatever It Takes to Get Whatever It Is You Want

If I decide that I am going to buy something or that I would like to get something, I know that I will have it in some future reality; I just haven't paid for it yet. The problem for most of people is that when they haven't paid for it, they decide they can't have it. When I haven't yet paid for something I ask: "Okay, what am I going to have to be or do to create this?"

QUESTION FOURTEEN: *What have I decided I wanted in my life that I was not willing to pay for that if I were willing to pay for it would actualize it as my reality?*

_____

_____

_____

_____

_____

What have you decided you were not willing to pay for that if you would pay for it, would actualize it? You have to be willing to pay for it! You have to look at it and say, "I'm going to have this. I know I haven't paid for it yet, but I'm going to have it."

People are always trying to find bargains. What would happen if you were willing to simply pay whatever it took to get whatever it is that you want? What you are not willing to pay for becomes the place you end up paying in a different coin.

In the 1930s, the Chinese were making rugs for export to the United States for the Art Deco market. They're called Nichols rugs and they're brilliant. I first saw them twenty years ago, and I thought they were the most beautiful things I had ever seen. I wanted them. Did I need to have one? No. Did I want one? Yes. Was I willing to pay? At the time I was looking at them, they were about $500 a piece. That was twenty years before I could afford one. Then they went up to about $1,700. Today they are up to around $3,500—and I have a number of them in my house.

> What have you decided you wanted in your life that you decided you were not willing to pay for that if you were willing to pay for it, would actualize it?

> Everything that is times a godzillion, will you destroy and uncreate it all? Right and Wrong, Good and Bad, POD and POC, All 9, Shorts, Boys, and Beyonds.

Those are your questions for chapter one.

In a few weeks, I suggest that you do them all again. And in a few weeks after that, go back and do them again. Do the questions ten, twelve, or fifteen times until you come to the awareness of "Wow! I have a totally different reality now!" That new reality will start to show up in your life in ways you would never have expected.

You have now lost all of your excuses. What's your justification for not doing these questions going to be?

WORKBOOK QUESTIONS
CHAPTER ONE

QUESTION ONE: *What am I refusing to be that if I would be it would create too much money in my life?*

_____

_____

_____

_____

_____

QUESTION TWO: *What would it be like if I had $100 million a year for all eternity?*

_____

_____

_____

_____

_____

QUESTION THREE: *How much doubt am I using to create the lack of money I am choosing?*

_____

_____

_____

_____

_____

QUESTION FOUR: *What would I have to charge in order for people to receive what I have to give?*

_____

_____

_____

_____

_____

QUESTION FIVE: Where have I refused to be the real source of change that eliminates the awareness of the limitation I have chosen?

_____

_____

_____

_____

_____

QUESTION SIX: *What have I made so appropriate about money that I can't have the fun and joy of money?*

_____

_____

_____

_____

_____

QUESTION SEVEN: *What have I made the definition of money that keeps me from having it, enjoying it, and creating beyond this reality?*

_____

_____

_____

_____

_____

QUESTION EIGHT: *What am I trying to create in order to prove I don't have to have too much money?*

_____

_____

_____

_____

_____

QUESTION NINE: *What have I defined money as that it actually isn't?*

_____

_____

_____

_____

_____

QUESTION TEN: *What's the greatest amount of money I can willingly be?*

_____

_____

_____

_____

_____

QUESTION ELEVEN: *What can I do or choose that will create greater possibility in the world right away?*

_____

_____

_____

_____

_____

QUESTION TWELVE: *What can I be that I am not being that if I would be it would exponentialize my receiving off the charts of this reality?*

_____

_____

_____

_____

_____

QUESTION THIRTEEN: *What have I chosen as the sum of what I can be, do, have, create, and generate that keeps me living in this reality rather than having my reality?*

_____

_____

_____

_____

_____

QUESTION FOURTEEN: *What have I decided I wanted in my life that I was not willing to pay for that if I were willing to pay for it would actualize it as my reality?*

_____

_____

_____

_____

_____

CHAPTER TWO

WHAT IF EVERYTHING WAS ABOUT THE POSSIBILITY AND NOTHING WAS ABOUT THE PROBLEM?

Most of us tend to look for the problem rather than the possibility, whether it's about money or anything else. We have a tendency to think, "I've got to handle this problem." But what if everything was about the possibility and nothing was about the problem?

With money, everything has to be about possibility, never about problem, because when you look for the problem, you will always create the problem in order to create the possibility.

People say, "Yeah, but if we don't have our needs met financially, it seems like a problem."

I ask, "Is it really possible that you cannot have your basic financial needs met? Or is that a lie you are buying from somebody else's universe?"

What Is the Purpose of Money?

A class participant who was doing these questions said, "I am becoming aware of where I have locked points of view about money into my body."

I said, "Everything that money is, is about your body and the way you use your body."

What is the purpose of money? Is it to facilitate you, the being? Or is it to facilitate *your body*? Does a being need a house to live in? No. Does a body need a house to live in? Yes.

Does a being need a car to travel in? No. Does a body? Yes. Does a being need clothes to wear? No. Does a body? Yes. The purpose of money is to facilitate your body.

You have to look at this and ask: "Is money making my body easier and is that going to create more?" We have created a separation between us and our bodies in order to create no money in our lives.

> Every lie you've bought in order to create a separation between you and your body in order to create no money, will you destroy and uncreate all those? Right and Wrong, Good and Bad, POD and POC, All 9, Shorts, Boys, and Beyonds.

QUESTION ONE: *Is money making my body easier and is that going to create more?*

_____

_____

_____

_____

We have the point of view that we are together with our body in this game of money, but actually it's our body that is in this game of money.

QUESTION TWO: *What part of the game of money am I playing with my body and what part am I losing with my being?*

_____

_____

_____

_____

We tend to think that we have our soul or our being, and we have our body, and our body should change and adjust according to our being, but that's not the way it works. If we were functioning with our body, we would be able to win the game of money with ease.

> Are you refusing to win the game of money with ease by separating from your body in order to create the loss of money in this reality? Everything

that is times a godzillion, will you destroy and uncreate it all? Right and Wrong, Good and Bad, POD and POC, All 9, Shorts, Boys, and Beyonds.

If you are playing the game of money with your body, you realize that the purpose of money is to make your body comfortable. Do you make your body comfortable with what you choose? Or are you trying to make you comfortable with what you choose?

Most people try to make themselves comfortable with what they choose. That's losing, because you cannot make you, the infinite being, comfortable. Infinite beings are not uncomfortable; they are expansive.

What you do with your life should be about making your body comfortable. For example, I have a really comfortable bed. I have a nice pillow top on it, and I have a three-inch orthopedic mattress with a four-inch down mattress on top of that. I love getting into my bed! You spend eight hours in your bed every day. It should be a really comfortable place.

Be somebody who wants comfort, because the body desires comfort. I've had people visit who would say, "Oh, no worries. I'll sleep on the floor." Why would you ever sleep on a frigging floor? There's a bed right here! I watch people who put their overweight bodies in Spandex. That can't possibly be comfortable. They do that because they think it makes them look good. It makes their being feel better to think they're making their body look smaller. What would it be like if you just allowed your body to be lighter because that is what works for it?

This is an acknowledgment of what is. Money is not the same for you as it is for your body. Do you, the being, need money? No. Do you, the body, need money? Yes. You, the body, like money. You, the being, don't care. Most people are not willing to recognize this. You aren't winning the game of possibility because you aren't looking for what's going to actually create a different possibility.

How much money are you using to validate the limitations of this reality that keep you from living beyond it? Everything that is times a godzillion, will you destroy and uncreate it all? Right and Wrong, Good and Bad, POD and POC, All 9, Shorts, Boys, and Beyonds.

What is it that you are not willing to tell yourself about money that if you would actually tell yourself about it would free you to have more money than you think is possible? Everything that is times a godzillion, will you destroy and uncreate it all? Right and Wrong, Good and Bad, POD and POC, All 9, Shorts, Boys, and Beyonds.

Have You Decided You Are Stupid with Money?

People often have reactions when they spend money. They say, "Oh! Now I won't have enough" or "This is all I have at the moment." They are functioning from a less-than-aware point of view, which is stupidity. You can ask: "How can I get more stupid than I currently am with money?"

The reason you have a problem with spending money, the reason you have a problem with having money, the reason you have a problem with anything to do with money is that you have decided you are stupid with money.

QUESTION THREE: How can I get more stupid with money than I currently am?

_____

_____

_____

_____

If you go to McDonald's because you think it must be good because it's cheap, a) you are an idiot, b) you are stupid, and c) you are insane. I'd rather go to a good restaurant and buy an appetizer for ten bucks than go to McDonald's and buy a hamburger, French fries, a cookie, and one of their malts for ten bucks. I would rather be satiated by the joy of eating than satiated by a full belly. Most people are trying to fill up what they call empty instead of creating what is possible beyond empty. Empty is the lie of this reality.

QUESTION FOUR: *What have I defined as a full belly instead of the satiation of possibilities that keeps me from hWaving the money I would truly like to have?*

_____

_____

_____

_____

Are you doing full belly instead of the satiation of possibilities? Everything that is times a godzillion, will you destroy and uncreate it all? Right and Wrong, Good and Bad, POD and POC, All 9, Shorts, Boys, and Beyonds.

Can you truly be empty? No. Can you be space? Yes. Have you defined space as *empty*, or *empty* as *lack*?

> Everywhere you have defined empty as lack, will you destroy and uncreate it all? Right and Wrong, Good and Bad, POD and POC, All 9, Shorts, Boys, and Beyonds.

> What have you defined as a full belly that is not satiation of possibilities? Everything that is times a godzillion, will you destroy and uncreate it all? Right and Wrong, Good and Bad, POD and POC, All 9, Shorts, Boys, and Beyonds.

Beliefs

People tell me that this reality requires an exchange of money for things. I ask, "Does this reality require an exchange of money? Or does this reality believe you require an exchange of money?" It believes you require an exchange of money.

> How many beliefs are you using to eliminate the money you could be choosing? A few thousand, a few billion, a trillion, a godzillion, or more than that? Everything that is, will you destroy and uncreate it all? Right and Wrong, Good and Bad, POD and POC, All 9, Shorts, Boys, and Beyonds.

Have you noticed that as you read that question, all kinds of weird energy comes up? Every belief requires you to take a weird energy and twist it into something it isn't, especially with regard to money. How many beliefs are you using to eliminate the money you could be choosing? Isn't it interesting that you like eliminating money from your life? You like not having it. Not that you would ever admit that.

Why would you do that? In order to believe that you can live like a finite being in a finite reality with a finite capacity and finite monetary flows, you have to eliminate total being.

> Everything that is times a godzillion, will you destroy and uncreate it all? Right and Wrong, Good and Bad, POD and POC, All 9, Shorts, Boys, and Beyonds.

Trying to Fit In

Someone told me that every time she did these questions, she kept coming back to limitations around trying to fit in and not stand out. All the limitations we have about money are about fitting in, not standing out, and not being different. The same person said that the things that were coming up for her were like an apology for existing.

> Everything you have done to take life as a literal transgression against being, will you destroy and uncreate it all? Right and Wrong, Good and Bad, POD and POC, All 9, Shorts, Boys, and Beyonds.

I said, "This is where you have to ask: 'And how much more insane can I actually be?' When you find yourself doing insane things and you say, 'Wow, that was insane!' don't try to stop the insanity. Ask: 'How much more insane can I actually be?'"

> What energy, space, and consciousness can I be to be out of control, out of definition, out of limitation, out of form, structure, and significance, out of linearity, and out of concentricity as money for all eternity? Everything that doesn't allow that to show up times a godzillion, will you destroy and uncreate it all? Right and Wrong, Good and Bad, POD and POC, All 9, Shorts, Boys, and Beyonds.

You keep trying to avoid that which will actually work in order to prove that your life doesn't work.

> What energy, space, and consciousness are you using to create the life that doesn't work you are choosing? Everything that is times a godzillion, will you destroy and uncreate it all? Right and Wrong, Good and Bad, POD and POC, All 9, Shorts, Boys, and Beyonds.

This is where you can't check out. You have to start to see what is true for you and what would create a different reality.

Money Problems Are Not a Reality

A lady told me that when she asked the question: "What would it be like if I had $100 million a year for all eternity?" she kept getting the answer that there'd be nothing to fix and nothing to dream for. There would only be death and despair.

I said, "If you had $100 million a year for all eternity, none of those things would matter. Then what would you like to create?" Monetary problems are the creation of a problem; they're not a reality. You create them in order not to have an ease about creating beyond anybody else's reality. It's like you don't want to live alone. You'd rather have a really bad relationship so you can feel screwed up.

QUESTION FIVE: *If I had no monetary problems, what would I create?*

_____

_____

_____

_____

_____

The lady I was talking with also said, "When I say that I would have nothing to dream for, there is also the element of no choice, because with $100 million a year, I couldn't be me. The money would be more than me.'"

Do you have a definition of you that defines you by the level of money you currently have? As long as money is more valuable than you, can you choose consciousness? No.

> Are you avoiding the consciousness you could be choosing by the money you are defining you can have? Everything that is times a godzillion, will you destroy and uncreate it all? Right and Wrong, Good and Bad, POD and POC, All 9, Shorts, Boys, and Beyonds.

QUESTION SIX: *What have I defined me as based on the money I currently have?*

_____

_____

_____

_____

_____

If you had to create your reality beyond anybody else's reality, what would occur? You'd have to get to a place where your brain goes out to lunch, and possibility begins to eat at the limitations of your reality so you start to create a reality that actually works for you. Be willing to be the awareness of those possibilities.

Ask: "What do I need to do or what do I need to be that would bring this to actualization with total ease?" You choose to be aware but rather than actually being aware, you keep trying to see that something else is necessary, something else is proper, or something else has to happen.

It's not "Something else has to happen." It's "What do I need to be or do to actualize this?"

A guy told me, "I can perceive the space I am being where I am asking for and inviting infinite possibilities, and then my mind goes to thinking about money. It goes to the numbers and how much I need to create. It just takes over. It's like an auto-responder. I don't know what to choose or change about that."

I said, "Your mind is always an auto-responder. That's all it is. Your mind doesn't know how to do anything but auto-respond. Why would you listen to it?"

He said, "Yeah, but how do I know how much to create?"

I said, "You are trying to come to conclusion. You're not trying to know."

He said, "That's true. So when I get the amount I'd like have to each month, do I just ask what it would take for that to show up?"

I said, "Yes. Ask: 'What can I be, do, have, create, or generate that would allow this to show up?'"

Do You Ever Ask the Consciousness of the Universe to Contribute to You?

The universe has your back when you ask it to send you what you need. You have to ask it to contribute to you. Do you ever ask the consciousness of the universe to contribute to you? You never do. You ask for some stupid person to come and tell you what to do. You ask for somebody who knows more than you. You ask for everything except the consciousness, which knows more than you do in every respect, to actually deliver. What would happen if you were willing to have that?

Someone said to me, "You've said that you've created a financial reality beyond what most people ever have. Is that where you know the universe has your back and more is coming—because the universe supports what you are creating?"

I said, "I know that I have my back and the universe will have it too, because I have it. I know I'm not willing to give up, and as long as I'm not, the universe won't either."

Money Is Something You Can Use to Change People's Reality

You've got to look at these things. If you are going to do anything with money, ask: "How is this going to change reality?" That's the question you should live as. Ask: "What is money going to create? What is it going to change?"

Today Dain and I had lunch at one of our favorite restaurants. The hostess there loves us. She smiles at us and takes care of us. When Dain comes in she becomes a very happy person. She looks at him with lust in her eyes. When I left today, I gave her a $40 tip. Nobody tips a hostess. It's just not done. Did I change her reality with a $40 tip? Absolutely.

Money is something you use to change people's reality. What amount of money can you use that would change somebody's reality? I've told the story a thousand times about going into a restaurant where I ordered a cup of coffee and a donut. The woman who served me was slow and uncertain. It was her first day on the job, and she'd never been a waitress before. She was having a difficult time. The bill came to $6. I left $12 on the table. She came running out after me as I was leaving, saying, "Sir, you gave me too much money."

I said, "No, that's an acknowledgment that you will do the job and you will survive and you will be fine. Worry not and you will be okay." The change in her world over six frigging dollars was dynamic. It was not the amount. It was the thought. In every moment, you've got to ask: "How can I use the money I have to create a different reality for someone right now?" You've got to be willing to look at that, because the purpose of money is not about having more of the stuff you think you need to own.

How Do You Want to Live Your Life?

Someone said to me, "In a short period of time, I've experienced being a multimillionaire and I've experienced bankruptcy, and I don't see what I did to have one versus the other."

I said, "It's not one versus the other. The question is 'Which one's more fun?' Being money has more ease than being poverty. It has more ease because it's more you. Most people don't want to get this. What if you were willing to be that level of money in life? What could you create as your reality?"

You have to look at how you want to live your life, because as you begin to create your life, the universe starts delivering to you. When I was young and dumb and had no money, I was often around an aunt who had lots of money. She had beautiful things, she had beautiful rugs, she had beautiful china, crystal, and sterling flatware that she ate with every day. That was her reality. I said, "I want to live like that!"

Did I have the money to do that? No. Did I know how I was going to get there? No. Did I know I wanted to live like that? Yes. I started going out and buying things for ten bucks that were worth more than that. I started creating a lifestyle with beautiful things in it that indicated where I wanted to go, things that someone would own if they had true wealth in their life. It was not about what I had; it was what I could have if I was willing to go there. Today I live in a house full of beautiful, museum-quality things.

You've got to be the guru of your own reality. You are the only superior being who is going to create the reality you're capable of creating. If you think somebody else can do it, you're insane. The one thing you are not willing to look at is "I am totally stupid, I am totally insane, and I am frigging crazy beyond my wildest reality."

That's what I am. But because of my insanity, my craziness, my outrageousness, because of all the things I am willing to be, I have created a financial reality that few people on the planet have. Try asking: "What energy, space, and consciousness can I be to be as stupid and insane and outrageous as I truly be?"

Creating Beyond This Reality

There's a way of creating on this planet in this reality which is based on conclusion.

It works up to a point but then there's a certain point at which it no longer works. That's why you have to create beyond this reality.

When I learned that conclusion was a way of stopping me, I said, "F--k this. I'm not going to conclude about anything. I am going to be in question about everything." I can say that 1,000 times, and you will never hear it. You will choose conclusion over possibility, always. You go back to a conclusion because you're not willing to ask: "What question do I have to be to create a different reality with total ease?"

You have to create beyond this reality. Conclusion works only as long as you are not willing to expand your life beyond anybody else's reality. Let's say you've got a million dollars. That's nice—but what is it going to change? Is $10 million going to change much? Not if you hold on to it. But is a different point of view going to change reality? Yes!

You have to choose. You have to say, "I'm not going to come to conclusion with this." People ask me to come to conclusion, and I say, "I see your point of view—and what else is possible? What haven't you considered? What hasn't occurred?"

Your choice, your awareness, and your point of view require no money. Your point of view can change reality; your money cannot. You've got to look at:

> What point of view can I have that would create a monetary reality greater than what I currently have with total ease? Everything that is times a godzillion, will you destroy and uncreate it all? Right and Wrong, Good and Bad, POD and POC, All 9, Shorts, Boys, and Beyonds.

QUESTION SEVEN: *What point of view can I have that would create a different financial reality for me today?*

_____

_____

_____

_____

_____

I was talking with someone who said, "Part of me gets frustrated because I'm not willing to do what it takes. I'm not willing to work forty-eight hours a day to make all the money I desire. It doesn't sound fun. I'd rather be out playing."

I asked, "What if what you did to create money was play? You don't want to believe it's possible to have fun with what you do to create money."

People look at what I do and ask, "How can you work as much as you do?"

I say, "Because it's fun!"

Dain was up till two o'clock in the morning last night, handling some things for our business. He grumbled but he enjoyed it. How do I know he enjoyed it? Because he kept doing

35

it when he had the opportunity not to. Grumbling is fun too. Complaining is fun. Do you get that? It's fun to kvetch.

Poisoning the Well of Possibility

When people tell you, "You can't do that," that's a poisoning of the well. When people say, "That can't be possible," that's a poisoning of the well. And the well is the lifeblood of possibility.

> Have you had people poison the well of possibility that you've never acknowledged? Everything you've done to somehow make that poisoning real, will you destroy and uncreate it all? Right and Wrong, Good and Bad, POD and POC, All 9, Shorts, Boys, and Beyonds.

We had an IT guy who was trying to create IT things for Access. He told me that what one of my friends had created for our IT element was total crap and absolutely unusable. Then he went ahead and used it for twelve months. I looked at it and said, "He's trying to poison me against her! Does that create more possibility or less possibility?"

When I realized that, did it create something different? Yeah. For one thing, it gave me my friend back. I didn't have to think that she had done something against me. People like the IT guy do this sort of thing to poison you against others.

> Everywhere that you've been poisoned against those who will create more possibility, will you destroy and uncreate it all? Right and Wrong, Good and Bad, POD and POC, All 9, Shorts, Boys, and Beyonds.

> How many times, how many places, how many forms and events of poisoning you against others have been done to keep you from having the brilliance of connection that will always support you? Everything that is times a godzillion, will you destroy and uncreate it all? Right and Wrong, Good and Bad, POD and POC, All 9, Shorts, Boys, and Beyonds.

Let's say that somebody tells you, "I think your wife is cheating on you." Is that poisoning the well of your affection? Totally.

If somebody tells you, "That person is not your friend," do you then say, "Yes, they are"? Or do you say, "Oh. I'm not sure" or "I've got to ask them about this"? Or do you create a separation from that person in order to believe that what was told to you was true?

When Dain first came into Access, people said to me, "He's going to steal all your clients and leave you in the lurch." I looked at it and said, "No, that's not true." Then I said, "Okay, steal my clients. Do I like them all enough to hold on to them? No. Feel free to steal them." And of course, Dain has stolen all my clients and gone away. Not.

You've got to be willing to look at something and say, "That's not true." Would your husband or wife cheat on you? Yes. Under what circumstance? Under the circumstances in which you poisoned the well of your own possibilities. The places where you are cutting off your awareness are the places you are poisoning the well of possibility.

I was talking with a lady who said, "My family was giving me money and I was receiving it and then they told me I was bad with money because I received the money. It's like they were poisoning the well of my receiving.'"

> How many poisonings of the well of your being are you using to limit your receiving? Everything that is times a godzillion, will you destroy and uncreate it all? Right and Wrong, Good and Bad, POD and POC, All 9, Shorts, Boys, and Beyonds.

Okay, this is the end of chapter two. Please do the questions from chapter one again. And then answer the following questions from this chapter.

WORKBOOK QUESTIONS
CHAPTER TWO

QUESTION ONE: *Is money making my body easier and is that going to create more?*

_____

_____

_____

_____

QUESTION TWO: *What part of the game of money am I playing with my body and what part am I losing with my being?*

_____

_____

_____

_____

QUESTION THREE: *How can I get more stupid with money than I currently am?*

_____

_____

_____

_____

QUESTION FOUR: *What have I defined as a full belly instead of the satiation of possibilities that keeps me from having the money I would truly like to have?*

_____

_____

_____

_____

_____

QUESTION FIVE: *If I had no monetary problems, what would I create?*

_____

_____

_____

_____

_____

QUESTION SIX: *What have I defined me as based on the money I currently have?*

_____

_____

_____

_____

_____

QUESTION SEVEN: *What point of view can I have that would create a different financial reality for me today?*

_____

_____

_____

_____

_____

TRUSTING YOURSELF

Sometimes people tell me that they don't trust themselves. But if you don't trust yourself, how are you ever going to have money or receive anything? When you buy the lie of not trusting you, you are also buying the lie of not trusting that the universe will contribute or the universe will provide. You're not willing to be part of the universe that can be trusted.

> What have you made so vital about never having trust in you that keeps you eternally seeking the necessity of destroying you and never saving you? Everything that is times a godzillion, will you destroy and uncreate it all? Right and Wrong, Good and Bad, POD and POC, All 9, Shorts, Boys, and Beyonds.

QUESTION ONE: *What part of the universe can I trust? And what part of me am I not trusting?*

_____

_____

_____

_____

When you start to look at those two questions, you'll get a lot of answers about where you are sitting. Do you trust yourself? Do you know who you are? No. Why? Because you are like a day. You are never the same twice. You change every day, so how can you trust yourself to be the same? You can't, and people don't like it when you are not the same. They want you to be consistent. They look at life from the point of view that what makes you trustworthy is never going outside the box and never being different. They don't trust you when you keep changing. Even if you are trustworthy and you have somebody's back, they won't be able to see it. They can only see that you're changing and they will conclude that you're not trustworthy.

It's a problem that you are trying to use other people's conclusions to determine what equals you. You doubt yourself because you perceive that the other person doesn't trust you. You look to change yourself so they will trust you, but you're constantly changing, so they never will.

Why would you want someone to trust you? Why would you not trust you? If you don't trust yourself, how are you ever going to have money or receive anything?

> What have you made so vital about never having trust in you that keeps you eternally seeking the necessity to destroy you and never save you? If you can't save you, you can't save money, because you have to be money in order to have money. Everything that is, will you destroy and uncreate it all? Right and Wrong, Good and Bad, POD and POC, All 9, Shorts, Boys, and Beyonds.

Power Does Not Come from Consistency

Most of us had parents who told us, "You have to be consistent." Do you really have to be consistent? No. What do you have to be? You have to be inconsistent. When you try to be consistent, you must sit in judgment of everything you do and choose.

Do you try to be consistent with money? Yes, and how does that work for you? It doesn't. You judge every penny you spend and every penny you make. You judge everything you do with money. Is that going to create more money? No. Your greatest judgment of you is that you are not consistent, yet your inconsistency is the greatest source of power for you, which is why you're trying to get rid of it. You don't wish to be powerful.

> What energy, space, and consciousness can you be to be as totally inconsistent as you truly be? Everything that is times a godzillion, will you destroy and uncreate it all? Right and Wrong, Good and Bad, POD and POC, All 9, Shorts, Boys, and Beyonds.

When I recently fired our counsel in the U.S., our counsel in Ireland got a little freaked out because they didn't know whether I was going to fire them as well. They are now more on their toes. Who has the power? We do. You have to be inconsistent; you have to be willing to change on a dime to create what is possible.

When I first met Dain, he was in a relationship that wasn't working out, and in one day, he quit and moved out. I loved that. That's the way I used to function before I got married. Once I had children, I thought I had to be consistent. The funny part is that when I stopped being consistent, my kids turned out to be far more adept at adjusting their lives than other kids. Consistency demands of you that you give up everything in order to have consistency. Inconsistency is the greatest source of power for you.

You look for what is consistent in your life, like your rent and your bills. Those are consistent. Do they have anything to do with you? Or do they have to do with what you have to pay? How much creativity, how much creative capacity do you use to pay for the things in your life that you have to deal with consistently? Those things are not about trusting you.

> How much of you have you given up to be consistent in your finances, your money, and your job for all eternity? Everything that is times a godzillion, will you destroy and uncreate it all? Right and Wrong, Good and Bad, POD and POC, All 9, Shorts, Boys, and Beyonds.

What's more important—to be consistent or to be aware? To be aware! What have you been choosing? Awareness? Or consistency?

QUESTION TWO: *Where am I being consistent in my life where I could be inconsistent, and what choice can I have that would allow me to be inconsistent?*

_____

_____

_____

_____

_____

Where Do You Spend Your Money?

Look at where you are spending your money, so you know whether that's where you actually want to spend it. Do you want to spend your money on a cup of coffee per day? Or do you want to create something else in your life that you haven't yet allowed yourself to have?

When I saw how much I was spending on coffee, I said, "Wait a minute. What I really want is to have more of this in my life," and I started to look for how I could create more of that. Slowly but surely, those became the things I would spend my money on. I cut down on the coffee and spent $20 a week buying something I wanted to have in my life, an antique or something that was going to be worth more than I was paying for it.

That's creating wealth from the point of view of asking: "What can I buy or do that is going to give me a greater return than anything else?"

Consciousness is possibility. What energy, space, and consciousness can create this? Start looking at everything you are trying to create and see whether it is actually working for you. Start functioning from this point of view, because if you don't, you are setting yourself up to lose.

Survival vs. Thrival

I talked with a lady who had accepted a new job. Before she took the job, she did a spread-sheet and saw that the pay would cover her basic expenses and probably not much more. She asked: "If I take this job, what will my life be like in five years? If I don't take this job, what will my life be like in five years?" Taking the job felt light and expansive to her, so she went for it. Then she started calculating how to keep her expenses less than the income that would be coming in, and that felt really contractive. She asked me, "How can I play in the possibilities here?"

I said, "You're looking for how to cut costs in order to live within your means. Does that have anything to do with creating a life? No. Somewhere along the way, you bought the idea that life is about survival and not about thrival."

Is this something you've done? Here's the question you need to ask:

QUESTION THREE: *Where am I trusting only to be able to survive, and where am I avoiding everything that would allow me to thrive?*

_____

_____

_____

_____

_____

I asked the lady who was trying to cut costs, "How many hours a day do you have to work at your job?" We calculated that she spent eight hours working, eight hours sleeping, two hours commuting, and three hours eating, taking care of her body, and getting ready for work. I said, "That leaves three hours in which you do what?"

She said, "I guess I just fritter away that time."

I said, "That is correct. You fritter away that time. You don't ask: 'How do I use this time to create more in my life—more money, more possibility, more choice, more of everything?' You have to get all of it. You are trying too hard to live a normal life. You need to ask: 'If I were willing to have all the money I could have, would I live my life from a normal reality?' No!"

Where are you creating your life as normal rather than infinite possibility? That's what you have to look at.

QUESTION FOUR: *Where am I creating my life as normal rather than a source of possibility?*

_____

_____

_____

_____

_____

If You Don't Make a Choice, Nothing Can Change

Choice is the most useful thing there is, because every time you make a choice, something occurs. How do you change something when you are not making a choice? You can't. If you don't make a choice, nothing can change.

It's important to make a choice whether or not you think it's going to work. The lady who made a choice to take the new job and then started looking at how it wasn't going to work went to the conclusion that she made a wrong choice, which meant that anything that was right about that choice could not come into her awareness. It could not come in to her life and create something greater for her.

Conclusion has nothing to do with creation. You have to look at something from the point of view, "I made a choice." For example, I made a choice for us to go with a certain IT solution. We got to the point where it was supposed to be finished before we discovered it couldn't actually work. Everyone started asking, "Oh my God! Should we actually do this?"

I said, "Yes. Go ahead and do it and we'll correct it to whatever degree is necessary. If we have to put it off for a little while and correct it, is it going to cost us more money? Yes. Is that right or wrong or good or bad or what? It just is."

I made the choice, and having made the choice, we got to the day it was supposed to be up and running, and it couldn't take the payments that were coming in. It couldn't do what we needed. We required a different solution, and we're now looking for that, whatever that takes, and we will find it.

I'm talking about the recognition that you have to look at something and ask: "Is this working the way I need it to? Yes or no?" If the answer is no, then do something different. You have to be willing to change on a dime. Most people are so concerned about being consistent that they will eliminate their creative capacity, yet the thing that creates the most money is your creative capacity.

> How much money have you lost in your need to be consistent? Everything that is times a godzillion, will you destroy and uncreate it all? Right and Wrong, Good and Bad, POD and POC, All 9, Shorts, Boys, and Beyonds.

Possibility, Choice, or Insanity?

What do you want to create as and from—possibility, choice, or insanity? It is just a choice. Most people choose the most insane things they can, thinking that's the way to create something.

> What have you made so vital about resisting the ease of creating and making money that keeps you seeking the difficulties instead of the possibilities in every choice? Everything that is times a godzillion, will you destroy and uncreate it all? Right and Wrong, Good and Bad, POD and POC, All 9, Shorts, Boys, and Beyonds.

I knew a guy who had $3,000 in his life. He said, "I really need to make money and I have a great opportunity to invest in something that's going to give me a 2,000% return."

I said, "Well, if you want to invest in that, feel free. That's not what I'd choose." Why wouldn't I choose it? Because if it's too good to be true, it's too good to be true. You have to be willing to look at what is—not what you would like it to be. I have watched too many people try to create things the way they "should" be rather than asking: "How can I create this in a way that actually works for me?"

You choose the most insane things to prove you have possibilities. You try to prove it's not an impossible choice, you try to prove it is the right thing to do, you try to prove all kinds of stuff. But little of it has anything to do with what is actually true.

If I were the guy who had $3,000, what choice would I make? I'd ask: "If I'm going to spend this, what can I spend it on that is going to create wealth? What's going to create wealth?"

Most people see possibility as the moment when they choose something that looks good on the surface, whether or not it will make them any money. They say, "This looks like a really good deal."

I don't do that. I ask, "Can I get a better deal than this?" What would happen if you were able, willing, or wanting to create a greater possibility, a greater result, and a greater choice?

You think you have to jump off a cliff to prove there are possibilities. You'd rather come to conclusion than jump to awareness. What about being pragmatic? What about choosing? What about asking a question? Before I buy something, I ask: "Do you have a sale on this suit?" "Can I get a better deal?" or "What's the best deal you can give me?"

What Do You Want to Create?

You have to look at what you are willing to create. What do you want to create? Are you willing to look at what you actually want to create? No. You just want to create something better than what you currently have.

A lady said to me, "I've been asking, 'What do I want to create?' forever. I truly don't know what I want to create. I just know that it's something different."

I said, "You're a humanoid. The only way you know what you want to create is by doing something until you know that you don't want to do it. You think that if you don't want to do something anymore, you're a failure. You're not a failure. You're a humanoid, but you have to be willing to be a failure; otherwise, you judge every choice you make as though the judgment and the choice based on the judgment are going to create more."

The problem with becoming an older humanoid is that what you don't want to create becomes apparent to you very quickly. You say, "Oh! I don't want to do this. What's the matter with me? Am I stupid? Oh yeah, I am. What's wrong with me that I can't decide what I really want to do?"

You'll do something for three weeks and then you're over it. You'll think, "What the hell? Did I really want to create that or not?" You created as far as you wanted to go with it and then you were over it.

Do you remember the first question in chapter one? "What am I refusing to be that if I would be it would create too much money in my life?" Are you willing to be a failure?

> What energy, space, and consciousness can I be that would allow me to be the absolute and total failure I truly be? Everything that is times a godzillion, will you destroy and uncreate it all? Right and Wrong, Good and Bad, POD and POC, All 9, Shorts, Boys, and Beyonds.

Going Beyond Your Comfort Zone

We were talking about knowing what you want to create in the Advanced How to Become Money class, and someone said, "At the end of my creations, there seems to be a judgment like, 'This is not enough.' I don't say, 'Woo-hoo! I did it. What else is possible?' I make myself wrong for what I created."

I said, "'This is not enough' is not a judgment. It's an awareness. You could ask: 'What could I create or generate that would be more than enough for me?' You are trying to create without going out of your comfort zone."

Your comfort zone is a place where you know "I can create enough. This is okay for me." You don't choose to go beyond that. What would it take to change this? Choice.

Ask: "What's the most uncomfortable thing I could choose to be today?" For example, you have to be willing to charge an amount for your services that makes you uncomfortable. What's valuable to you? What's your time worth to you?

For a while I was charging $1250 an hour for private sessions. People would call me and cry, "Oh, my life sucks! Blah, blah, blah." Do I want to listen to that crap? No. So I asked, "How much would I have to charge so people would go directly to the point and we could deal with it?" I changed my hourly rate to $2500. Now, at $2500, ninety-five percent of my sessions only go half an hour instead of an hour. People don't go to all their tears and stuff anymore. They go directly to what they want to handle. I'm not making a lot more money, but don't have to listen to all that other stuff. It works for me.

Are you willing to ask, "What's my time worth to me?" Or do you say, "I know the amount is way more than I am comfortable charging." Find out what your time is worth to you and you'll get clients who are comfortable with spending that kind of money. Think about tripling your rates. Or maybe you want to ask: "What energy, space, and consciousness can I be, to be totally poverty-stricken and living on the streets for all eternity?"

Are you willing to live on the street? No? Okay, then, you have to charge!

You may be one of those people who conclude, "Well, people won't pay me that much," or "I'm not worth that much." What question is that? It's not a question! It's a conclusion—and if it's a conclusion, can anything else come into your reality? Nope!

Do you want to change your conclusion or do you want to change your reality?

What Do You Desire?

Or you may be one of those people who are so snobbish, you won't ask for money. You say, "Oh, well, I don't really need it." That's called, "I'm such a snob that I'm going to be homeless on the street so I can be superior to everybody by being homeless."

Some people equate asking for more money with begging. They're so elite, they would never ask for money. Yet they'll say, "Fix me, Gary, I want a different reality." When I give them a way to fix themselves, they say, "Oh. I'm too big a snob to do that."

What are you not being that would give you everything you desire? You don't even know everything you desire because what you desire is not a cognitive universe. You think that once you have it figured out, once you have it cognitively actualized, everything will turn out fine. But that's not the way it works. When we got involved in creating our center in Costa Rica, I didn't have a clue about how we could pay for it. We got involved in it anyway, and we finally made the first payment on the land. We are actually on the way!

When I was talking about how we did it and all the things we had to work out, someone said, "Gary, of course you can do that. That's who you are. But we're talking about me now."

I said, "You've got to use the question: 'What am I not being that would give me everything I desire in life?'" I'm willing to be everything in life, do anything, have anything, create anything, and generate anything because I don't have the point of view that I can't. I am also aware of the fact that every time we make a choice, the universe opens up fifty-five doors for us to look in. But you never look in."

Looking in is asking: "If choose this, what is this going to create? If I choose this, what is this going to create? If I choose this, what is it going to create?" It's about your choice. It's not about the result you're looking for.

I'm being what will create and generate more consciousness. You're looking at how much money you are going to make. That is never my criterion, and what happens is that I seem to make more and more money.

Money is a by-product of your choice. Choice does not create money. Money comes as a result of choosing.

You Create Awareness by Every Choice You Make

The only way your life is going to be satisfactory to you is if you seek to create a greater life. A couple of years ago, I had a conversation with a friend about seeking to create a greater life.

She asked me, "Is Access going the way you want?"

I said, "No, it's not growing fast enough."

She asked, 'Well, how much money are you making?"

I said, "About a million and a half a year."

She asked, "Is that enough for you?"

I said, "Sure, it's enough for anybody. I'm comfortable."

She asked, "So what would you have to be making for it to grow the way you want?"

I said, "A lot more!" I upped it to a minimum of $10 million a year and then to $100 million a year. In the two years since then, Access has gone from forty-seven countries to 183 countries. What does that tell you about how the universe supports you?

People tell me they are seeking a greater life, yet they judge what they choose to get there. I ask, "Are you actually judging it? Or are you creating awareness by every choice you make? You think you're judging it—but in actuality you're recognizing, 'Oh! That's not where I want to go.'"

If you were walking across a field and you made a choice to turn right and there was a giant hole, would you fall in it? No. You'd say, "Wait a minute. This isn't working. What choice do I have here that could change this?" It's always about choice.

Please do the questions in this chapter and keep doing them so you start becoming aware of what is true for you. I'm asking you to have fun with money. What would having fun with money look like? It would look like a lot more fun than you're having!

WORKBOOK QUESTIONS
CHAPTER THREE

QUESTION ONE: *What part of the universe can I trust? And what part of me am I not trusting?*

_____

_____

_____

_____

QUESTION TWO: *Where am I being consistent in my life where I could be inconsistent, and what choice can I have that would allow me to be inconsistent?*

_____

_____

_____

_____

QUESTION THREE: *Where am I trusting only to be able to survive, and where am I avoiding everything that would allow me to thrive?*

_____

_____

_____

_____

QUESTION FOUR: *Where am I creating my life as normal rather than a source of possibility?*

_____

_____

_____

_____

_____

CHAPTER FOUR

SEX, MONEY, AND RECEIVING

People often tell me that they desire friendships with others, but instead of creating friendships they seem to create separation, which stops their receiving. I'm going to start this chapter with a question that's going to mess you up—but first I want to say something about receiving and sex.

Sex is the lower harmonic of receiving. It is a limited version of receiving, just as thoughts, feelings, and emotions are lower harmonics of knowing, perceiving, and being. So if you avoid sex, or you don't like sex, or don't want to have sex, or you won't have a certain kind of sex, or you see sex as something bad instead of something that's a possibility, you cut off the possibilities of receiving money as well as sex.

Sex is the human point of view about receiving. If you are having sex, you are receiving. If you are not having sex, you are not receiving. Does that mean you have to have sex? No. Does that mean you could have sex? Yes, if you choose it. It's got to be a choice. It's the same thing with having money; it has to be a choice you make.

For example, do you avoid the idea of sex with children? Does asking that question that mean I want you to go out and have sex with children? Absolutely not. But if you don't see that kids are sexual and you don't see that kids are willing to have sex, you have to cut off your own awareness to make that work, so that you can't receive money from children.

Your children can be a source of money. If you ask them to contribute to your making money, it's amazing the energy that they can contribute that creates money in your life. You've got to be willing to have it all.

> What have you made so vital about never having sex that poisons the well of being in order not to have money? Everything that is times a godzillion, will you destroy and uncreate it all? Right and Wrong, Good and Bad, POD and POC, All 9, Shorts, Boys and Beyonds.

QUESTION ONE: *Where am I avoiding sex in order to avoid money?*

_____

_____

_____

_____

_____

Sex Has Nothing to Do with Copulation

These are things that have to do with sex but nothing to do with copulation. What does that mean? Sex is an energy in your body, and your body is the one that needs money. Try this: Ask your body, right now, to exponentialize the blood flow in the genital areas of your body. And again. And again. And again. Do you notice any changes going on with your body?

Do you notice any pain in your body? Pain may come up when you ask your body to do that because of all the places you have resisted the sexual energy that greater blood flow would give you.

> What have you made so vital about never having sex that poisons the well of being in order not to have money? Everything that is times a godzillion, will you destroy and uncreate it all? Right and Wrong, Good and Bad, POD and POC, All 9, Shorts, Boys and Beyonds.

People talk with me about their sexual need, and I've asked, "Well, why don't you just pay to have sex?"

They say, "I would never do that!"

I say, "You would never pay to have sex. That means you would never pay to receive. You will not pay to receive money either, will you? What if you had to spend money in order to make money?" Do you get the correlation here?

You create orders of the day in your life where you don't get to have money. The order of the day is "no money." The order of the day is "no sex." The order of the day is "no receiving."

What part of sexual need have you cut off in order to not to receive money and to have money left out of your life? Everything that is times a godzillion, will you destroy and uncreate it all? Right and Wrong, Good and Bad, POD and POC, All 9, Shorts, Boys and Beyonds.

A lady in a class said, "Over the years the more stuff I have cleared out using the tools of Access, the more I don't have a point of view about whether I have money or don't have it, or whether I have sex or don't have sex. I don't really care about it. Yet, I desire it. It's kind of a strange place to be."

I said, "It's not a strange place to be. It's the way it should be. You've got to let it come the way it comes. You've got to allow it to be what it is. If you truly wanted to have sex, could you get it?"

She said, "Of course. Any time."

You can have a desire to have sex and you can have a desire to have money, but what choice would you have to make to actualize it? Desire is always about a future reality. It's not a necessity of anything now.

I never cut off my sexual energy and I also know what it creates, so I don't choose to go there with people when I know it won't work out well. I realize that my sexual energy is a contribution to me in my life and I am willing to look at and see what the choice will create. I ask: "What choice can I make that would create money right away?"

QUESTION TWO: *What sexual choice could I make today that would make money for me right away?*

_____

_____

_____

_____

_____

It's about the receiving. It's not about the copulation. I can have sexual energy. I can appreciate sexual energy. I can flirt. I can be romantic. I can do all those things, but I am also aware of what's going to happen if I go there. You have to be willing to know what the result will be if you choose it. This is not about being indifferent to sex, copulation, or money; it's about having no necessities. When you get to the point of view that nothing is a necessity, everything becomes choice.

For example, you may know that if you cheat on your partner, it's going to be a disaster. But you go ahead and have sex with someone else because you need that to feel good about yourself. You are not actually cheating on your partner; you are trying to find you again. That's a different reality. Most people, instead of asking, "What do I really want to create here?" go to "I have to have sex." You don't have to have sex. You would like to have sex. You're alive; you'd like to have sex. Does that mean you are going to have it the way it should be, the way it ought to be? Not necessarily.

I have a friend who sells $5,000 worth of product a day, minimum, after he has sex. So every time he's feeling funky about his business, I tell him, "Go have sex." Recently he has noticed that as soon as he starts to think about having sex, he starts to sell stuff too. This is the place you have to get to—the sense of "How am I going to create money? What energy do I need to be?"

> What energy, space and consciousness can you be to have more money than God for all eternity? Everything that is times a godzillion, will you destroy and uncreate it all? Right and Wrong, Good and Bad, POD and POC, All 9, Shorts, Boys and Beyonds.

The Motivating Factor

Do you become uncomfortable when you think there isn't enough money? It should make you uncomfortable. You associate the thought "never enough" with worry and anxiety. But "never enough" is not worry and anxiety. "Never enough" is the necessity of creation. People misidentify and misapply worry and anxiety, not as creation, which is what it is, but as some kind of necessity that must run their life. That sense of necessity becomes their motivating factor.

> What have you misidentified and misapplied as a motivating factor that isn't a motivating factor that if you didn't misidentify it as a motivating factor would allow you to create greater than you have ever been willing or able to create? Everything that is times a godzillion, will you destroy and uncreate it all? Right and Wrong, Good and Bad, POD and POC, All 9, Shorts, Boys and Beyonds.

> Where have you misidentified and misapplied the ability to choose and create something greater than you've ever been able to choose or create as anxiety and worry? Is that the lie you are using to cheat you from the money you could be choosing? Everything that is times a godzillion, will you

destroy and uncreate it all? Right and Wrong, Good and Bad, POD and POC, All 9, Shorts, Boys and Beyonds.

The feeling of lack is not real. Can an infinite being truly lack? No. Can an infinite being truly worry? No. Can an infinite being have anxiety? No. So what the hell are you making yourself out to be? A cardboard figure of a humanoid reality?

QUESTION THREE: *Where have I identified myself as a cardboard figure that I have played paper dolls with continuously throughout my entire life?*

_____

_____

_____

_____

_____

You create yourself as a paper doll, somebody you stick clothes on, and then you drop the paper doll into the world and say, "See you later." If you make yourself a cardboard figure, do you make yourself a pile of shit?

QUESTION FOUR: *Where have I made myself a powerless pile of shit that keeps me from having more money than God?*

_____

_____

_____

_____

_____

Does God have any money? Does God need money? Does God always get whatever He wants? So why don't you? God is always knowing that you will get whatever you want if you just decide you are going to go for it.

What have you misidentified and misapplied as a motivating factor that isn't a motivating factor, that if you didn't misidentify it as a motivating factor would allow you to create greater than you have ever been willing or able to create? Everything that is times a godzillion, will you destroy and uncreate it all? Right and Wrong, Good and Bad, POD and POC, All 9, Shorts, Boys and Beyonds.

Go to Question

People sometimes tell me, "When I begin to offer a service or a class, I start to have expectations and conclusions about how many people will show up for it and how I will facilitate the event."

I always say, "You've got to get to question. The moment you come to conclusion, you've completed the whole thing, and you can't get the money."

There was a man who was doing Access. He had twelve people sign up for a class he was giving, and he said, "This is so great! I'll be able to pay all my bills and do blah, blah, blah."

I thought, "Big mistake," but he didn't ask me a question, so I kept my mouth shut. When he showed up on the day of his class, and only one person was there. Twelve people had signed up, but only one came. The guy called me and asked, "What did I do?"

I said, "You started spending the money before you got the money. You spent it before it came in."

When you deal drugs, you know that nobody is buying your product until they show up with the money. You never count on selling your product; you wait until someone hands the money to you. When you deal in drugs, you never give anything up until you get the money.

Well, you're dealing the drug of consciousness. You have nothing to sell and you have nothing to give and nobody is going to take what you have until they show up with the money in their hand. If you do otherwise, you are spending your fortune before you make it.

> What have you made so vital about spending your fortune before you make it that makes sure you'll never actually have a fortune? Everything that is times a godzillion, will you destroy and uncreate it all? Right and Wrong, Good and Bad, POD and POC, All 9, Shorts, Boys and Beyonds.

QUESTION FIVE: *What projections, rejections, expectations, judgments, and separations do I have that are creating my current financial and clientele situation?*

_____

_____

_____

_____

_____

QUESTION SIX: *What projections, rejections, expectations, judgments, and separations am I using to avoid the money I could be choosing?*

_____

_____

_____

_____

_____

Projections and expectations are what you think someone else will do even if they aren't going to do it. A projection would be "This man is perfect for me." An expectation would be "He will have the same point of view about me that I have about him. He'll think I'm perfect for him."

Judgment is any fixed point of view or any conviction that someone or something has to be a certain way. Separation occurs once you do a judgment of any kind. You separate yourself from the person or thing you judge—even if it's you. Rejection is dismissing or refusing something.

Whenever you are doing projection and expectation of any kind, you are separating, judging, and rejecting anything that would give you awareness. You're eliminating your awareness.

Your projections and expectations of what is occurring or what should be occurring are creating the limitation of what's showing up right now. Projections, rejections, expectations, judgments, and separations aren't going to get you anywhere. All they get you is no income. When you have little to no income, you've got to ask this question:

QUESTION SEVEN: *What choice am I making to have the money I currently have and no more?*

How Can You Change the World by the Way You Use Your Money?

I would like to create $100 million a year. Why? Because I want to be rich and famous? No. Because I am rich and I want to be more rich and more famous? No. It's because I want to see what I can do to change the world, and money is one of the many things you can use to change the world.

It's not about the amount you spend to create a change. It's about the amount of money you have and how that can change the world. I've told the story a thousand times about leaving a six-dollar tip for a six-dollar snack. You have to look at a situation and ask: "What do I really want to create here? What's really possible?" In this case, a six-dollar tip changed a woman's life. Did that change the world? Yes. With every tip you leave, you use money to change people's lives. You change the world. You can change people's lives with five bucks or fifty bucks or 100 bucks. You can change the world with whatever it is you have in your pocket that's available.

> Money is a tool you can use to create a different reality. Are you using it in that way? Everything that doesn't allow that to show up, will you destroy and uncreate it all? Right and Wrong, Good and Bad, POD and POC, All 9, Shorts, Boys and Beyonds.

QUESTION EIGHT: *What can I do with my money today that would change the world right away?*

QUESTION NINE: *What can I be or do today that would make money easy for me always?*

"Can I Have Some Money, Please?"

A lady told me she was hosting a class at her home, and after the class, a five-year-old girl who loves visiting her asked, "Can I have a lollipop?"

The lady said, "I don't have any lollipops in my house, but I have some chocolate."

The girl said, "I want a lollipop. Can we go look in your basket?"

So they went upstairs to look in the basket and there was no lollipop. Then all of a sudden, the girl said, "Look! I found one!" and she pulled a lollipop out of the basket—and then a second one—and said, "See? You have lollipops."

The lady, who swears those lollipops had not been there previously, said to the girl, "I adore the way you create."

Kids are willing to be everything and receive everything. They're willing to be infiniteness. What about us?

The little girl said, "I want a lollipop." Do you ask for more money that way? Do you say, "I want money"? Or do you ask, "What am I going to do to get the money?"

I say, "Okay, I need some more money. Can I have some more money, please?" It's like kids. They look at you and ask, "Can I have some more of this, please?" and you say, "Sure."

If you were the universe and a little kid asked you, "Can I have more of this?" you'd say, "Yes." But you act like the universe doesn't respond the way you would. What if you were being totally clean and asked, "Can I have some money, please?" Would the universe respond to you exactly the way you would respond to a little kid?

A friend of mine had some passes to the aquarium and took his son. As they walked in, the kid asked, "Can I get a toy, Dad?" The dad reached into his pocket and realized he hadn't brought his wallet, his credit cards, or any cash. He just had the passes. He said, "We're going to have to find somebody we know to get the money from."

They walked into an elevator and the kid said, "Let's go to the third floor, Dad," and he pressed the third-floor button. The door to the third floor opened and there was a ten-dollar bill on the ground—the money for the kid's toy. Done!

Will you make your life that easy? Nope, you've got to make it hard.

People tell me, "You make it sound so easy."

I say, "It is easy."

They say, "Well, it's not easy for me!" Is that your point of view too? Do you realize that you do not desire it to be easy? I once asked a class, "What would happen to your life if it was too easy?"

A lady said, "Oh! Everything would be so easy. It would be lovely!"

I said, "It would be lovely?! What about having an outrageous life? Notice that you didn't say it would be exciting or it would be fun. Lovely is a word you use for a nice dress. You choose a lovely dress; you don't choose lovely money. You want a lovely life instead of a fabulous life. You don't even want a fabulous dress that knocks people's socks off when you walk into the room. You have to get over this point of view that you want to live a lovely life.

Are you refusing to have the outrageous life you'd actually like to have?

Everything that is times a godzillion, will you destroy and uncreate it all? Right and Wrong, Good and Bad, POD and POC, All 9, Shorts, Boys and Beyonds.

You have to look at what your point of view is. What's your point of view about money that keeps you from having it? Get rid of the idea that it would be *nice* or *lovely*.

Money Comes with the Specificity of What You Want to Create

What are you going to have to be or to do, to get what you really desire? You're going to have to get specific if you are going to create money. Money comes with the specificity of what you want to create. What about asking, "What am I going to have to be or do to have the fabulous life I truly desire?"

Personally, I love beautiful things. I've seen a lot of people who have beautiful things in their houses, but in most of those houses, you can't use any of the beautiful stuff. You can't sit on any of the furniture. There are little ropes across the couches because they are museum quality. I now have a house that has that kind of stuff. Do people sit on my couches and chairs? Yes! My point of view is if you ain't using it, why have it?

A participant in the Advanced How to Become Money class said, "My mum used to put plastic on our sofas."

I said, "You need to take the plastic off of your life. You have plastic over your own life right now so it doesn't get dirty, so it will look lovely, no matter how many times you sit on it, but as long as it has plastic on it, you can't ever really touch it. What if you touched your life?"

Do you put plastic on your sofa? Where are you plasticizing your reality so you don't have to touch it?

QUESTION TEN: *Where am I plasticizing my life so I don't have to touch it or be involved in it?*

_____

_____

_____

_____

_____

Things have to get messy. If you are going to have an outrageous life, if you are going to live beyond the pale. If you really want to have money, you have to be willing to live messy. That doesn't mean you have a messy household; it means you get to mess everybody else up who doesn't keep it straight for you.

You've got to be willing to mess up people's lives because people want plasticized lives where nothing ever touches them.

I had a maid who was going so frigging slow. I said, "I'm not paying $20 an hour for somebody to work this slow. I'm cutting your wages back to $12 an hour." Now she's grateful for the job. She comes in and gets everything done faster. I don't know how that's happening. She's thrilled she has the job. She thanks me daily for having her here. What? How's that the way it works? Because that's the way it works. People cannot have greater than what they are willing to have.

QUESTION ELEVEN: *What have I decided I am not willing to have that's greater than what I am willing to have?*

_____

_____

_____

_____

_____

Once when I was talking about having a messy life, someone said, "When I interact with people, I feel like I alienate them."

I said, "Yeah, isn't that fun?"

She said, "It's horrible. I hate it."

I said, "No, you don't! If you really hated it, you wouldn't do it." When you alienate people, they can't get close to you. It's called plasticizing your life. That's the way you can keep your plastic world. You don't want to reach into the depth of the possibility of what you could create now, because if you did, you would have to outdo yourself."

Please answer the following questions again. And take that plastic off your furniture and your life!

WORKBOOK QUESTIONS
CHAPTER FOUR

QUESTION ONE: *Where am I avoiding sex in order to avoid money?*

_____

_____

_____

_____

QUESTION TWO: *What sexual choice could I make today that would make money for me right away?*

_____

_____

_____

_____

QUESTION THREE: *Where have I identified myself as a cardboard figure that I have played paper dolls with continuously throughout my entire life?*

_____

_____

_____

_____

QUESTION FOUR: *Where have I made myself a powerless pile of shit that keeps me from having more money than God?*

_____

_____

_____

_____

_____

QUESTION FIVE: *What projections, rejections, expectations, judgments, and separations do I have that are creating my current financial and clientele situation?*

_____

_____

_____

_____

_____

QUESTION SIX: *What projections, rejections, expectations, judgments, and separations am I using to avoid the money I could be choosing?*

_____

_____

_____

_____

_____

QUESTION SEVEN: *What choice am I making to have the money I currently have and no more?*

_____

_____

_____

_____

_____

QUESTION EIGHT: *What can I do with my money today that would change the world right away?*

_____

_____

_____

_____

_____

QUESTION NINE: *What can I be or do today that would make money easy for me always?*

_____

_____

_____

_____

_____

QUESTION TEN: *Where am I plasticizing my life so I don't have to touch it or be involved in it?*

_____

_____

_____

_____

QUESTION ELEVEN: *What have I decided I am not willing to have that's greater than what I am willing to have?*

_____

_____

_____

_____

_____

CHAPTER FIVE

WHAT DO YOU WANT TO DO WITH YOUR LIFE?

Here's the thing about creating money: You are a humanoid. You don't actually care about money, and without a purpose for having it, you won't ever have it. However, if you could see what you would do if you had $100 million, you could start to create $100 million to do what you'd like to do. You need to have a purpose for having money.

What do you want to do with your life? That is the reason for asking, "If I had $100 million, what would I do with it? What would I create?"

Creating Beyond This Reality

You have to get to the awareness "I'm not actually creating my life." Then you can ask: "Is this where I really want to live? Or do I want to do something different? And if I were doing something different, what would I do?" But it's not really about what you would do; it's what would you be. What would you have to be to have a different reality than the one you currently have?

> What would you have to be to have a different reality than the reality you currently have? Everything that is times a godzillion, will you destroy and uncreate it all? Right and Wrong, Good and Bad, POD and POC, All 9, Shorts, Boys, and Beyonds.

I was talking with a lady who said, "If I had a $100 million, I don't think I'd want to create anything. I'd just want to experience this world and travel and have adventures, but I have resistance to trying to figure out how to get the money to support that." Her point of view was "I don't want to have to make money. I just want to be able to go play."

I said, "You have been buying into all of this reality's choices and not choosing for you. If you want go around and see the world, that's this reality. What would you create if you were creating everything you want?"

That's being the energy of creating beyond this reality. There are so many more choices! How many more choices could you have if you were truly having your choices? What choice would you make if you were choosing for you? This is where you can ask: "What choice am I making to have the money I currently have and no more?"

Please ask yourself this question:

QUESTION ONE: *What have I made so vital about choosing from the menu of this reality that keeps me from having my reality?*

_____

_____

_____

_____

_____

A lady who was about to fly to the U.S. to do the Conscious Horse, Conscious Rider class called me and said, "A taxi is coming in four hours to take me to the airport. I really want to take this trip, but everything in this reality is screaming at me not to go. 'It's not practical. Think of your family, your in-laws, your finances.' There is a pattern to this. I do things that are inconceivable to other people. I see things I could be or do different, yet there is a part of me that still buys into this reality."

I asked, "What are you trying to create from? Awareness? Conclusion? Or the rightness of somebody else's point of view? How much of your conceivable universe belongs to other people?"

She said, "I'm aware I have a different choice than everybody else. I'm aware that I'm willing to make choices for things that are inconceivable, but this reality is taking up way too much of my time at the moment."

Does this describe you? You have to ask: "What is it I want to create? What is the most important thing for me in my whole life that if I could create it, would make me happy?" Do you actually choose what makes you happy? Or are you trying to make other people feel comfortable and happy?

Why is it an issue for you that other people don't have the point of view you do? If nobody agrees with you, do you have to see the rightness in their point of view? Why do you even care why they choose what they choose? Why do you care about their point of view? Because you're supposed to? That's called "Somebody else's sanity must be greater than mine, because I know I am insane." You think they are going to put a little white jacket on you and carry you away. Don't come to a conclusion about what you choose. Ask a question.

QUESTION TWO: *If there was no conclusion about what I was choosing, what would I create?*

_____

_____

_____

_____

_____

You keep trying to see whether the choices you made were bad or good. But if you are trying to see whether your choices were bad or good, you cannot see what they created. You can only see the judgments other people give you.

You make a choice and you say, "That wasn't my best choice." But then instead of asking, "What else can I choose?" you start looking for how you were right or how you were wrong.

The Strength You Are

What if you were never right? What if you were never wrong? There would be only one thing left that you could be—totally strong. If you're never right and you're never wrong, the only thing left is to be totally strong, because strength comes from the awareness of the difference you are, not from the judgment of other people's realities about what to choose.

Most of us do not acknowledge the strength we have and are. How does it become acceptable to you to never acknowledge the strength that you are?

QUESTION THREE: *What strengths am I not acknowledging?*

_____

_____

_____

_____

_____

Strength is a place where you know you cannot be broken. Is there someone who has tried to break you? Have they succeeded? No. Can they bend, fold, staple, and mutilate you? Only to the degree that you allow them to. You don't have to make that person right. You don't have to make that person wrong. You just have to be strong.

What makes you stronger than other people? It's having no judgment or point of view, especially about you. When you can do that, you are stronger than anybody else.

QUESTION FOUR: *Write down five things you've decided you are, or five characteristics you have. Then look at each thing and ask: Is this wrong or is this strong?*

_____

_____

_____

_____

_____

Characteristics are a choice you have made and then solidified as though that is all you are, as though you aren't everything else as well.

QUESTION FIVE: *Now write down five things you think are really wrong about you. Then look at each one of them and ask: Is this something wrong or is this something strong I have not been willing to acknowledge?*

_____

_____

_____

_____

_____

The best thing about you is what you think is wrong about you. For example, do you think you're bad with money? You have to see how the opposite is also true of you. If you can be one side of the coin, you can also be the other side. You can live on the edge of the coin and you get to flip-flop back and forth anytime you want. You have to be willing to see the strongness and not look to the wrongness.

QUESTION SIX: *Look at each item you've written down in answer to Questions Four and Five.*
- *Ask: What's the opposite of this? Write down your answers.*
- *Ask: Am I capable of being the opposite of this too? Write down your answers.*
- *Then ask: If I am willing to be this and the opposite of it, what kind of strength can I have and be? Write down your answers.*

_____

_____

_____

_____

_____

Recognizing the Strength

I recently found out that the people I hired to handle a lot of financial and legal stuff for us managed in the last year to run up a bill of three-quarters of a million dollars in legal fees and finance charges. I don't make myself wrong for not having seen it before they made a mess. I simply take that awareness, choose something that works for me, and then do it.

It's not about seeing something instantaneously before it becomes a mess. It's about recognizing the strength that a mess shows you're capable of dealing with. What are you capable of dealing with that other people can't? And what if it's not really a mess? What if it's something that gives you a sense of self that you cannot get any other way?

I was aware that those people could give us some information we needed, and we got that. I was enthralled with what they could provide, not what they would provide. Next time I will look at what somebody can and will provide.

To be honest, I'm grateful it happened. We can go on now in a way we couldn't before. Was any part of it wrong? No, it was part of how we got to the awareness we want to have. I want total awareness. I don't care what it takes to get it. I don't care what I lose to get it. You've got to get to the place where you're willing to look from that point of view.

Doing "Pathetic"

Someone said, "Sometimes it seems like being pathetic is more valuable than acknowledging the strength that I am."

I said, "That's because you have managed to get a lot out of being pathetic. When you do pathetic, people give you things, they take care of you, and they run errands for you. That's why pathetic seems more valuable. It works. The question is: 'What do you want to occur?' It's not a wrongness to be pathetic. It's a great tool. It's a way to mess with people."

I'll be pathetic when I need to be pathetic. I'm really good at pretending I'm having a terrible moment. When we were registering people for the Conscious Horse, Conscious Rider class, I said, "I don't know how to do this on my phone. I don't know whether my phone does this. Can you do this for me, please?"

The person I was talking with said, "You have to stop pretending you believe the shit you are putting out to us about how you are incompetent with technology. We have watched you do too many things that are not incompetent."

I said, "Wow, I've blown my cover."

Rather than acknowledging the strength, you are always looking for the weakness and making the weakness wrong. You don't ask: "With this weakness, how am I strong? If I am doing pathetic, how is that a strength for me? What am I creating with that point of view?"

Can't you see how brilliant you are? You can do pathetic at exactly the right moment and get other people to do exactly what you want them to do. It's just a choice. Choose what works for this ten seconds. It doesn't matter what you choose. It doesn't matter!

Who Are You Going to Trust?

The lady who was about to get on a plane for the Conscious Horse, Conscious Rider class said, "There is no good reason for me to get on a plane and go to the States in four hours; however, my awareness is that I cannot afford to not go to the airport in four hours."

I asked, "So who are you going to trust?"

She said, "Me!"

You can make a full commitment anytime you choose. The question is: Do you make a full commitment to you?

Do you say, "I feel safe in taking this next step. Maybe I am going to fall off the cliff, but I always know I have a lifeline"? Do you know that you have a lifeline, whatever it is, even if it's your own strength? Or do you say, "Oh my God! I've got nothing! What am I doing this for?"

QUESTION SEVEN: *If I had no lifeline, what would I be?*

_____

_____

_____

_____

_____

Creating the Future Ten Seconds at a Time

The lady who was about the catch the plane knew that by going to the Conscious Horse, Conscious Rider class, her life was going to get better even though she had no bloody clue how that was going to work.

Most of you have the point of view, "Well, if doing this is about creating money in the future, I can do it, but if it's not for future money, I can't."

I don't do that. I ask: "If I choose this, what's my future going to be like? If I don't choose it, what's my future going to be like?"

Even with the people who took us for three-quarters of a million dollars, I knew we were creating a future. Then there was a certain point at which I said, "Okay, this is not creating the future. It's not going in the direction that the future we'd like to have can actualize. Something has to change. Something has to be different here."

When we became aware that something had to change, we did what it took to change it. You have to be aware of when it's time to change. You have to be aware of when it's time to do something. Don't function from the idea that anything is right or wrong or good or bad. It's just what it is.

The moment you go into the rightness or the wrongness, you kill the future. The moment you go into mistake and difficulty, you kill the future. You have to look at something and ask: "Okay, where do I go from here? Where do I go from here that maintains a greater future than I even know is possible?"

You simply are where you are, and you've got to go to someplace else. It's not "I've got to get it right," or "I've got to make sure I don't make this mistake again," or anything like that. It's "I know where I've got to go and I'm willing to go there."

You've got to ask: "If I didn't create the wrongness and the badness and the judgment, how quickly would what I desire actualize in my future?" That's the next question on your list, because you've got to stop going to the wrongness and rightness.

QUESTION EIGHT: *If I didn't create the wrongness and the badness and the judgment, how quickly would what I desire actualize in my future?*

_____

_____

_____

_____

_____

You start down a direction, and if it doesn't turn out the way you think it should, you go into judgment of it, which then destroys the future you created.

A good friend of mine says, "It never looks like what you think it's going to look like." If it's going to be different than what we think it's going to be, what is it going to be?

This touches all those places where you thought you had to create something or do something and you start asking, "Oh my God. What did I do wrong?"

What you did wrong was you decided that you did something wrong—and the future ended at that moment. We spend more of our lives ending our futures than creating the possibilities of them.

Getting Around the Insurmountable Object

You put mountains in the way of the future you are trying to create. In order to get rid of the mountains, you have to alter the way you do things.

If the mountains are there, they are your creation. What if they were yours to destroy as easily as they were created? The difficulty is most of us don't want to see that, because if we saw it, we'd have to believe in somebody we don't believe in—ourselves.

You see an insurmountable object and you think the insurmountable object is actually real. I look at it and ask, "How do I get around this?"

The insurmountable object is the thing you need to get around, not the thing you need to get over. What if there was nothing to get over, only everything to get around? But you don't think you're that good, do you? I think you're that good, but you don't. You have the ability to choose things other people can't choose, but you keep acting as though that's wrong, or that somehow you're wrong, or that something else has to occur.

I look at where I am. I am in the present. I ask, "Where do I have to go? What do I have to do today? What has to be handled?"

Making Other People More Important Than You

Have you found that very few people in your life are actually interested in you? Most of them only want to talk about themselves. Why is that? Because they're stupid! Stupid people always talk about themselves; they're not interested in you at all. An intelligent person is interested in everyone, which, by the way, means that most people are not intelligent. When people are not interested in you, it's because they're not intelligent.

You refuse to see this. You conclude that if someone is not interested in you, it means they're greater or more important than you are. Important means superior to you. People have told me they make others greater or more important because of their careers, or their money, or because they seem kind or hospitable, or some other thing. Why are you trying to make someone else greater or more important than you?

If you make people more important than you, they will create against you. For example, I made our counsel more important than I was because I thought they knew things I didn't know. Did they know things I didn't know? No. They had information I didn't have. That's different. It doesn't mean they knew more than I did or that they were more important than I was. I was looking at the information they could give me and seeing that as so important that I had to put up with what they were doing. I was willing to not see what they were doing because I had made them so important. All of us have done this. None of it makes us wrong. It just makes us a little myopic.

Making someone valuable is different from making them important. Valuable equals someone who is going to give to you. I have people who work for me. Are they capable of doing what I do? No. Is that significant? No. It doesn't matter whether people are capable of doing what I do. What matters is that they do what I need them to do to make my life work. If someone does that—if they are willing to do what I need them to do to make my life work—that person is valuable in my life.

I consider the maid who cleans my house and changes my sheets to be extremely valuable. She is a contribution to my life. Why? Because when I go into my room and see that my bed is made and it looks like a million dollars, is that helpful? Absolutely. Who you have decided is not valuable cannot create with you. They can only create against you.

QUESTION NINE: *Who am I not making valuable in my life that if I made them valuable would create more in my life?*

_____

_____

_____

_____

_____

WORKBOOK QUESTIONS
CHAPTER FIVE

QUESTION ONE: *What have I made so vital about choosing from the menu of this reality that keeps me from having my reality?*

_____

_____

_____

_____

_____

QUESTION TWO: *If there was no conclusion about what I was choosing, what would I create?*

_____

_____

_____

_____

QUESTION THREE: *What strengths am I not acknowledging?*

_____

_____

_____

_____

_____

QUESTION FOUR: *Write down five things you've decided you are, or five characteristics you have. Then look at each thing and ask: Is this wrong or is this strong?*

_____

_____

_____

_____

_____

QUESTION FIVE: *Now write down five things you think are really wrong about you. Then look at each one of them and ask: Is this something wrong or is this something strong I have not been willing to acknowledge?*

_____

_____

_____

_____

_____

QUESTION SIX: *Look at each item you've written down in answer to Questions Four and Five.*
- *Ask: What's the opposite of this? Write down your answers.*
- *Ask: Am I capable of being the opposite of this too? Write down your answers.*
- *Then ask: If I am willing to be this and the opposite of it, what kind of strength can I have and be? Write down your answers.*

_____

_____

_____

_____

_____

QUESTION SEVEN: *If I had no lifeline, what would I be?*

_____

_____

_____

_____

_____

QUESTION EIGHT: *If I didn't create the wrongness and the badness and the judgment, how quickly would what I desire actualize in my future?*

_____

_____

_____

_____

_____

QUESTION NINE: *Who am I not making valuable in my life that if I made them valuable would create more in my life?*

_____

_____

_____

_____

_____

CHAPTER SIX

WEALTH AND FORTUNE

I know a lady whose great grandfather came to the United States from Ireland in the late 1800s. He went to Texas and he asked, "How can I get land?"

He said, "I can make saddles. That's the one place where I have an ability," so he made saddles and traded them for plots of land, which were really cheap at the time. There was lots of land. It was Texas; it was big, and he ended up with over 80,000 acres.

Creating a fortune is about the capacity to see what's possible and then saying, "Okay, I'll do that." This guy applied his ability to create a fortune. He was willing to be a fortune.

Being a fortune is recognizing that whatever shows up in your life can be used to create something greater, so he made saddles and traded them for land. From there he traded saddles for cattle. From there he bought more cattle, and he continued on to create a fortune. He created a space for a possibility that others could not see.

A lot of Irish people came to the United States at that time to seek their fame and fortune, and many of them found it. If you don't seek your fame and fortune, you cannot find your fame and fortune.

Are you willing to be a person who has a fortune? Or are you only willing to be a person who has to work hard for his or her money?

> What have you made so vital about working hard for your money that keeps you being unfortunate rather than having a fortune? Everything that is times a godzillion, will you destroy and uncreate it all? Right and Wrong, Good and Bad, POD and POC, All 9, Shorts, Boys and Beyonds.

These days we have the point of view that fortunate people are just lucky. We think some master stroke of luck took care of them, but really, most people who are willing to have a fortune will be and do something greater than other people are willing to be and do.

What Could You Do If You Had a Fortune?

Do you desire a fortune? And if you had a fortune, what would you do with it? Right now, here in Texas the lottery is worth $450 million. I said, "Four hundred fifty million dollars! What could I do with that?"

Most people have the point of view that winning the lottery would mean, "I wouldn't have to work, I wouldn't have to do this, I wouldn't have to do that." They only look at what they wouldn't have to do; they don't look at what they could do if they had a fortune.

> If you had a fortune, what could you do that you are not currently doing? Everything that is times a godzillion, will you destroy and uncreate it all? Right and Wrong, Good and Bad, POD and POC, All 9, Shorts, Boys and Beyonds.

People who are creating fortunes look from the point of view of "What can I create with that?" There's no limitation in what they are willing to be. When you have a fortune, you have to be willing to be whatever it takes to create a fortune, like the saddle maker who was going to be the best damn saddle maker he could be. I would like to find one of his saddles. It would be fun just to feel the energy of this guy!

Never Wait, Always Create

I had a conversation with a woman who has been on "wait" for her fortune to arrive. She said, "For the past two years, I've been working on a project with the government that will create a fortune for me. Four months ago the papers got signed; however, I won't receive any money until a formal announcement is made, and the announcement isn't coming."

I said, "You have to call them and say, 'I thank you for doing this, but you guys aren't paying and you aren't making the announcement. I'm going to move on to other things, but I will still hold you to your contract.'"

She said, "Well, I've called some people and they keep saying, 'You need to wait for this announcement.' This announcement equals a fortune for me."

I asked, "Why are you putting your life on wait instead of going out and creating? Never wait, always create. I never wait for anybody or anything to come to fruition. I go out and create, and things come to fruition. Start on your next project if you need to. What else can you find that can create money? Waiting around for somebody to make an announcement?

Come on, they may make it, but if you sit there and wait for two years, you'll starve to death and die before you make any money."

She didn't get it. She kept saying, "But this equals a fortune for me…"

I said, "You're saying, 'This project is the source of my fortune.' No. This project is not the source of your fortune. You are the source of your fortune!"

Never wait. Always continue to create. You cannot rely on one thing to bring you your fortune. Fortune never comes from one source. It comes from the universe and your willingness to create it. Don't put all your eggs in one basket. Don't assume there's only one place fortune can come from. Fortune comes from what you personally are capable of creating. If you are capable of creating one source of a fortune, how many other sources of fortune are you avoiding?

> How many sources of fortune are you avoiding to create the limited financial reality you currently have? Everything that is times a godzillion, will you destroy and uncreate it all? Right and Wrong, Good and Bad, POD and POC, All 9, Shorts, Boys and Beyonds.

You, as a humanoid, have the ability to see fortune. You have the ability to hear it lightly knocking at the door, but you have made yourself deaf.

> Everything you have done to deafen yourself to the light knock of fortune, will you destroy and uncreate all that? Right and Wrong, Good and Bad, POD and POC, All 9, Shorts, Boys and Beyonds.

Choosing the Challenge vs. the Easiest Thing

I've talked many times about the antiques that come to me. I get chances to buy antiques and I look at them and I say, "Yes," "No," "Yes." It's an opportunity for me to make some money.

When I talk with people about this, they say, "Yes, but…" Why is there a but on your yes? If you're not willing to have every door open and choose every possibility available, you are creating a place where you can't have rather than a place where you can have.

Everything that is times a godzillion, will you destroy and uncreate it all? Right and Wrong, Good and Bad, POD and POC, All 9, Shorts, Boys and Beyonds.

I was talking with someone who said, "There was a point in my life where things came pretty easily, and I chose the challenge. I chose challenging work and a challenging husband I have since divorced. It was challenge, challenge, challenge. It's easy for me to look at the wrongness of those choices. What can I do to leverage the ability to create challenge in order to create wealth?"

I said, "Obviously you'd rather have a challenge than a fortune. Which is easier to get? A challenge or a fortune?"

You think a challenge is the thing that makes you work harder. But that's just working hard for your money. It's not having a fortune. The easiest thing for the saddle maker was to make a saddle. That was a piece of cake for him.

> What have you made so valuable about working hard for your money that keeps you unfortunate instead of somebody who has a fortune? Everything that is times a godzillion, will you destroy and uncreate it all? Right and Wrong, Good and Bad, POD and POC, All 9, Shorts, Boys and Beyonds.

> What energy, space and consciousness can you be that will allow you to choose the easiest way to create a fortune for all eternity? Right and Wrong, Good and Bad, POD and POC, All 9, Shorts, Boys and Beyonds.

Was it easy to get what you thought was a fortune when you were a kid? If you've got a hundred bucks when you're a kid, you think you've got a fortune—and for a kid, a hundred bucks is a fortune.

> What do you do that is a piece of cake for you that you won't use to create a fortune? Everything that is times a godzillion, will you destroy and uncreate it all? Right and Wrong, Good and Bad, POD and POC, All 9, Shorts, Boys and Beyonds.

A friend said to me, "I love making cookies, and I make good cookies. But as someone who has worked with mental health and depression for twenty years, I judge making cookies as less than doing work in mental health."

I said, "God knows a cookie never changes anybody's universe—or does it?" I knew a delightful lady years ago when I was in real estate in Santa Barbara. Her name was Debbie. She would bake all kinds of cookies and treats for her open houses. Her desserts were so good that other realtors would ask her, "Can I get you to make some cookies for my open house? I'll gladly pay you." After six months she was out of real estate and creating her own business, Debbie's Delights. Today it's a wholesale bakery with annual revenue over $50 million. The judgment that making cookies is less than something else is a way to avoid making a fortune.

I asked the lady who wanted to make cookies, "Are you are not willing to eat the sweet treat of life?"

She said, "I would feel guilty having things be so easy."

I said, "I suggest you give up that poverty line to prove how brilliant you are in order to survive poverty! I double dog dare you."

> I double dog dare you to live with a fortune, to overcome the challenge of having a fortune. Everything that brought up for you times a godzillion, will you destroy and uncreate it all? Right and Wrong, Good and Bad, POD and POC, All 9, Shorts, Boys and Beyonds.

Fortune Finds You—If You're Willing to Have It

Someone asked me, "What's the difference between finding a fortune and creating a fortune?"

I said, "You don't *find* a fortune. You create a fortune. Fortune finds you—if you are willing to have it. I am willing to have a fortune, but some people think they need an excuse to have one. If you are willing to have a fortune, things begin to find you. An example of that is all the antiques I've bought for little to no money that turned out to be worth massive amounts. I know a guy who has real estate come to him the way antiques come to me. You have the awareness and the information about the antiques or the real estate or whatever it is, and those things find you.

I learn about antiques and I ask them, "Are you worth more than I am paying for you?" When I started out, I didn't have any information about them. I just saw that something was pretty. You've got to look at things from a different direction than anybody else. I recently saw a collection of Chinese items for sale in Santa Barbara. It was great-looking stuff. I loved it. I asked it, "Are you worth more than I am paying for you?" It said, "Yes," so I bought it. It turned out that one piece was worth what I paid for the whole set. Did I know that upfront? No. Did I find out? Yes. I am willing to go to people who know more than I know and find out what they know.

I've also done real estate, so I know a little bit about that too. I've seen all the ways people can make money in real estate. I've made money from real estate for others. I've made other people a fortune, but I didn't make a fortune for myself. Why? At the time I wasn't willing to be the guy who had a fortune. You have to be willing to ask for the fortune, you have to be willing to have the fortune, and you have to be willing to trick yourself into having it by justifying all the reasons why you need it.

Fortune is the thing everybody says they want and it's also the thing they vilify. It's something they want; it's something they lack, but they are not willing to do whatever it takes to get there. If you have to make a hundred saddles to get there, are you going to do it?

QUESTION ONE: *What can I trick myself into doing today that will make me a fortune right away?*

_____

_____

_____

_____

_____

Stimulating the Competitive Edge of Your Reality

A lady asked me about her partner. She said he was creating a fortune but he was not willing to acknowledge it and to know his value.

I gave her the question: "What can I do to stimulate his competitive edge every day?"

She said, "I think I've been doing that without asking that question, and in some ways it's not a kindness to him. It just stirs him up."

I said, "Some people have to be stirred up to create more, and you've got to be willing to do that."

QUESTION TWO: *What can I do today to stimulate the competitive edge of my own reality right away?*

_____

_____

_____

_____

_____

You don't stimulate your *business*; you stimulate *you*. You're the only one you can beat. I can't beat anyone else; I can only beat me, because I'm the only one who has all the tools I have. I'm the only one who has everything I have. I'm the only one who knows where I'm not being totally confident.

Do you always settle for less than other people's perception of wealth, fortune, or money? That's because you hate competition. You won't let yourself have the best because you are trying to avoid competition. That which you hate is what you will create. When you hate competition, you will create it, and that will be the killer which keeps you from receiving the abundance of what you can have.

I will have the best and demand that people get better with what they choose. I love it when people come to my house and say, "You've inspired me to create more in my life."

When you choose the best, when you choose to be over the top, when you choose to have whatever you desire in life, you inspire others to believe they can have what you have. But you have to realize they will want to compete with you and have what you have.

QUESTION THREE: *If I was totally confident and capable of creating a fortune, what would I choose today?*

_____

_____

_____

_____

_____

Receiving the Results of Creation

We choose things like struggle instead of confidence. What is confidence? It's "Yeah I can do that." You choose to struggle over and over again because you have the idea that you don't have confidence. If you had confidence, you'd have no struggle, unless, of course, you like struggle. Which do you like better—confidence or struggle?

One day back when I was struggling as a real estate agent and making fortunes for other people rather than myself, I diligently looked at my situation. I was bluntly honest with myself. You have to be bluntly honest with yourself. I said, "This is insane. I just made $400,000 for a client by doing this deal for him—and I made $10,000 for myself. How come? Because he has the money to do the deal, he can make $400,000 and because I have the ability, I make $10,000. That's nuts. How can I change this? What can I be and do different that would change this around so that I am the one making $400,000?"

Blunt honesty is knowing what works. It's seeing what is, not what you want it to be. Most of you are not willing to look at your situation with blunt honesty. You say, "Well, I can't do that because I'm not confident," or some other thing like that.

Look at your life. I guarantee you there is some place where you made somebody else a load of money by what you know, what you did, or the way you are. Does that mean that they're the source? Or are you the source?

You have to be willing to be the source. You have to be willing to be the source of creation, and you have to be willing to be the receiver of the results of creation. Are you willing to receive the fortune that goes along with being the source?

> Everywhere you have decided you cannot be the receiver of the results of creation, will you destroy and uncreate all that? Right and Wrong, Good and Bad, POD and POC, All 9, Shorts, Boys and Beyonds.

Most people are not willing to be the source and to receive the results of what they create, but they will compete with themselves or with another in order to create something. That they will receive.

Other people refuse to compete. They lose interest when they have to compete. One guy asked me, "Why would I stimulate myself to a competition?"

I said, "Because that which you hate is what you create. It's a place where you cannot receive, you cannot be, and you cannot achieve."

This is also part of being bluntly honest. If you think, "I hate that," and you're honest, you'll recognize, "Oh. I'm hating this." You'll ask, "How is this going to work to my benefit?"

That Which You Hate Is Also a Source of Create

When I was a kid in the 1950s, my mother had colored aluminum drinking glasses. She thought they were great because they wouldn't break. I thought they were ugly. I hated them.

Recently I've seen those glasses selling for as much as ten dollars apiece and I've asked, "Why would anybody pay ten bucks for those ugly things?" But if I'm at a garage sale and I see six of them for twenty-five cents each, I'll buy all six and sell them to somebody else for a dollar apiece. I'll make some money on them. They can make me money because some people think they're beautiful or cool or retro. That which you hate is also a source of create.

Creating with Someone

Sometimes people ask about how Dain and I work together and how we've been able to create Access to be so much greater. Together we create more than either of us can separately.

If you're going to create with somebody, choose to create with them from the point of view of a) How can I outcreate them? and b) Are we more together than we are apart? You've got to be willing to outcreate the person, and they have to be willing to outcreate you too, which is their competitive edge, so the two of you are doing leapfrog all the time.

Ninety-nine percent of people in the world do not desire to create with other people. You may think someone wants to create with you and you may assume they are creating with you. But are they? You don't ask: "What does this person really want to create?" and "Is that the same thing I want to create?" You've got to look at what people are actually willing to create. Don't try to create from what you think they want. You have to look at what they truly want and create from there.

Don't assume they want to create from the kingdom of we[3] because that's what they say they want. I never believe anything anybody says. I question everything people say, because ninety-nine percent of the people lie to themselves every day, and they lie to everybody else eighty-eight percent of the time all day, every day. There's a twelve percent chance of truth coming out of anybody's mouth. If someone is speaking, chances are they are lying.

The only way you can tell whether someone is lying or telling the truth is by looking at what they produce. What they do determines the difference between what they say and what they create. Always pay attention to what somebody does—never to what they say.

We could all use some blunt honesty here because there's stuff we're not seeing.

QUESTION FOUR: *Where am I not being bluntly honest with myself and lying myself out of a fortune today?*

_____

_____

_____

_____

_____

QUESTION FIVE: *What would I have to be or do different so that I can receive as much or more than someone else can by what I create?*

_____

_____

_____

_____

_____

Would you like to create a fortune? Please answer all of the questions in this chapter—and go back in a week or two and answer them again, so you start becoming aware of what is true for you.

---

3. When you choose from the kingdom of we, it's not about choosing for you and against the other person. Nor do you choose for you and exclude the other person. You choose for you and everybody else; you choose what will expand all possibilities, including your own. When you do this, people around you realize their choice will expand by your choice, and they will contribute to your choice, not resist it.

WORKBOOK QUESTIONS
CHAPTER SIX

QUESTION ONE: *What can I trick myself into doing today that will make me a fortune right away?*

_____

_____

_____

_____

_____

QUESTION TWO: *What can I do today to stimulate the competitive edge of my own reality right away?*

_____

_____

_____

_____

_____

QUESTION THREE: *If I was totally confident and capable of creating a fortune, what would I choose today?*

_____

_____

_____

_____

QUESTION FOUR: *Where am I not being bluntly honest with myself and lying myself out of a fortune today?*

_____

_____

_____

_____

_____

QUESTION FIVE: What would I have to be or do different so that I can receive as much or more than someone else can by what I create?

_____

_____

_____

_____

_____

CHAPTER SEVEN

ENTHUSIASM FOR LIVING

Dain and I recently had an interesting talk with the financial advisor we've hired to work with us. He is very sane about money. He said, "I have the awareness of what you need to do regarding your taxes. I get that. But I can't speak to the awareness of what's going to happen with regard to your future creation of income." So we started to talk with him about that.

He said, "Very few people have enthusiasm about their future possibility of income. The enthusiasm you have about the money you can create is beyond anything I have ever seen."

For us, it's always about greater possibilities. Dain and I are always asking, "What else? What else?" You've got to look for greater possibilities, always. You need to ask: "What enthusiasm do I need to be in my life to create the future monetary reality I would like to have?"

The Joy of Creation, the Joy of Choice, and the Joy of Possibility

When you are enthusiastic, you seek out that which will work rather than that which will stop you. Most people don't do this. They tend to seek out a solution to their problem. They ask, "What's going to solve this? They think that if they can get unstopped, they will be able to create, but they lack enthusiasm for the joy of creation, the joy of choice, and the joy of possibility. Those are the things that create enthusiasm in life—joy, choice, possibility.

The question "What else?" is the form, structure, and significance that creates possibility. "What else?" looks at a greater and more enthusiastic reality than "What's going to solve this problem?" Those three elements, joy, choice, and possibility, create that which will give you enthusiasm, which is an innate quality you need in order to invite money to your party.

QUESTION ONE: *What enthusiasm can I be to create a totally different reality for me?*

_____

_____

_____

_____

_____

Enthusiasm Is Not Excitement

Enthusiasm and excitement are not the same thing. Enthusiasm is enjoying the moment and not projecting or expecting anything of it. Enthusiasm is not projections and expectations about how things should turn out, how they are going to turn out, or how they ought to turn out. Enthusiasm creates all forms of forward motion. It is "I wonder what this is going to look like!" Enthusiasm does not require you to complete anything. It is an ongoing explosion and experience of possibility. As Dain says, "It's a ball of light that comes from within and infuses itself into your life." It's a humanoid trait.

> How much energy have you used to suppress your innate capacity for humanoid enthusiasm? Everything that is times a godzillion, will you destroy and uncreate it all? Right and Wrong, Good and Bad, POD and POC, All 9, Shorts, Boys, and Beyonds.

Enthusiasm is being in an enthused position. A lot of people go to excitement rather than enthusiasm. They say, "I'm so excited about this!" Excitement means to be out of, not to be in. It is born of projections and expectations. You project and expect what something will create rather than seeing what is actually possible. Any projection or expectation, any "Oh, this going to be so good!" is a guarantee that things are going to be so bad.

Excitement is the projection and expectation you think you have been asking for. What does excitement do? It turns a possibility into an opportunity, and that's not what you want. Opportunity appears just before possibility opens the door—and it stops you from moving forward. You can get blindsided by too much excitement regarding your projections and expectations about what is possible, because any projection creates a blind spot.

What Else Is Possible?

I've been looking at the possibility of buying a ranch here in Texas because I have so many horses in California and it's costing me a ton of money to keep them there. Dain and I went out to look at property. I said, "We can buy some undeveloped land and put something on it." So we went out and looked at undeveloped land, and I said, "Wow, these people are selling bare, ugly land. They are selling what they don't want to live on. They have decided it's not of any value."

They are like people who have horses and function from what is called culling, which is getting rid of the ones you consider to be rejects. You choose based on rejection. This is not where you create possibility. Have you ever done rejection as a source of creation?

> Everywhere you've done rejection as a source of creation, will you destroy and uncreate all that? Right and Wrong, Good and Bad, POD and POC, All 9, Shorts, Boys, and Beyonds.

As Dain and I were looking at various properties, we were asking, "What else is possible here?" You can take something and you can turn it into whatever you decide to turn it into. You have to be willing to see what is available to you in every moment. That is what creates a sense of enthusiasm.

We looked at a property and we made an offer on it. I said, "Oh! We owe so much in taxes. How can I do this?" and then I talked to somebody who said, "Moving your horses to Texas could save you $6,000 to $8,000 a month. It would reduce your outflow, which would increase your income and your net worth. Why wouldn't you do it?"

I said, "Oh! I'm worrying about the taxes. I have to look at this possibility. Will the IRS confiscate the ranch? No, they don't do that. Will they be upset with me? Who cares?"

Who knows what is going to get created based on what you choose? You have to see that every choice is is going to create something. It's "What will occur as a result of this choice?" not "This is what I need to do because...." Every time you do "because," you are refusing to look at possibility. You are stuck in opportunity.

Most of you are not enthusiastic about what you are going to create. You say, "Oh my God, I wonder if this will work. Oh my God, will that work?" You have more "Oh my Gods" than "Wow, that's so cool. What else is possible?"

The key to being enthusiastic is being needless. When you are needless, you can have enthusiasm for whatever shows up in your life that can create more. If you are needy, you are always looking for money as a solution rather than a possibility. When you are needless, you have choice. When you have need, you must choose based on whether something is going to fulfill that need. Being needless is a lot more fun because you have choice.

Being the Question Generates Enthusiasm and Possibility

Being the question is part of what generates enthusiasm, and because question opens the door to everything, you begin to know what is possible by the choices you make. If you have a sense of question, then every time you make a choice, you see what gets created. But if you think you've got to get it right, you make a choice to see whether you got it right or wrong. It's never about the joy of creation, it's never about the enthusiasm and everything you get to choose.

Having something that you expect or having only one outcome you are looking for is the trap of death. You kill the things that create life—the enthusiasm and the joy of creation, possibility, and choice.

> Everything you have decided that allows you to get rid the joy of choice, the joy of enthusiasm, the joy of living, and the joy of possibility, everything you have done to choose something that will get rid of that, would you please revoke, recant, rescind, reclaim, denounce, renounce, destroy, and uncreate everything you have decided you have to have in order to have that as your reality? Right and Wrong, Good and Bad, POD and POC, All 9, Shorts, Boys, and Beyonds.

QUESTION TWO: *Where have I bought that my life has to be miserable instead of enthusiastic?*

_____

_____

_____

_____

_____

Committing to *You*

I had a conversation with a guy who said he was stuck in not committing to himself. He said, "I'm really good at creating distractions in my life. When I sit down to do something, I create a distraction or an excuse so I don't have to do it. I start to do things but I can't complete them."

I said, "You are actually very committed. You are committed to creating excuses and never completing anything."

He said, "I would like to change that."

I said, "You can't."

He asked, "I can't?"

I said, "You won't."

He said, "I would like to."

I said, "That's nice. You won't."

He said, "I will."

I asked, "Oh yeah? You sure?"

He said, "Yes."

I asked, "Swear on a stack of Bibles? Swear on the teachings of Buddha?"

He laughed kind of sheepishly and said, "I would not say yes."

"No Matter What It Takes"

I said, "You are more committed to failure than you are to success. You are more committed to stopping yourself than making yourself go. If you really want to change this, you've got to demand of yourself 'No matter what it takes, no matter who I lose, no matter what occurs, I am changing this. Enough. This is insanity.'

"Every time you sit down to do something and you make an excuse, say: 'Enough. I am not going to have an excuse anymore. My excuses are gone. I am now completing this,' and then make yourself do it.

"If you want this to work, you have to choose to make yourself do it. It is a choice you have to make. The only person in the world who makes you do what you don't want to do is you. You desire not to do it far more than you desire to do it. Isn't that clever? You say, 'I'm changing this,' and then you frigging change it!

"You are willing to commit to almost anything else, but not to you. You're not stuck at all. You are sticking yourself. You just flat out refuse to do anything. You are a refusenik."

A refusenik was a person in the former Soviet Union who was refused permission to emigrate, in particular a Jew who couldn't immigrate to Israel. It is also a person who refuses to follow orders or obey the law, especially as a protest. It's a person who is not comfortable with the system or who won't comply with the law because of a moral conviction.

> What are you refusing to be that you could be, that if you would be it would change your entire financial reality? Everything that is times a godzillion, will you destroy and uncreate it all? Right and Wrong, Good and Bad, POD and POC, All 9, Shorts, Boys, and Beyonds.

Please look at this. There's only one person who can stick you. You! Nobody else can stick you. You are the only one who has that kind of power. Why is that power more important to you than the power of creation, receiving, and enthusiasm? It's like you are stuck so you can be unenthusiastic about your life. You're not willing to change everything in your life.

> Who or what are you refusing to lose that if you lost them would allow you to have too much frigging money? Everything that is times a godzillion, will you destroy and uncreate it all? Right and Wrong, Good and Bad, POD and POC, All 9, Shorts, Boys, and Beyonds.

QUESTION THREE: *What have I done to make myself a refusenik today?*

_____

_____

_____

_____

_____

There Is a Different Possibility in Life

You have to get that there is a different possibility in life. Years ago when I was in the upholstery business, I went to a lady's house. She wanted to redo her entire house. She said, "I'm redesigning my house. I'm ninety-two years old and I may never finish it, but I want to have a good time while I'm doing it."

I thought, "Wow!" I asked, "What are you doing these days?"

She said, "Well, I get up at five in the morning and I spend an hour reading. After that I go outside and I work with my gardener in the garden for two hours and then I come inside and I meditate for a while and then I go back outside and look at everything. I am so grateful for what nature has given me. Then I get dressed and I go pick up my friends—they are all too old to drive anymore—and we have lunch." She was ninety-two and she was driving them. Her enthusiasm for life and living was extraordinary!

Someone told me, "I have enthusiasm, but I feel like it's dripping from a broken tap. How I can turn it into the waterfall of enthusiasm?"

I said, "Keep asking: 'What energy, space, and consciousness can I be to add more flow to my life with total ease?'"

Most of you would rather suffer life than be enthusiastic about it. You have to commit to your own life. Enthusiasm is when you are committed to your own life. You generate it from that choice. You cannot have a life that you are not committed to and have enthusiasm for living.

A participant in the Advanced How to Become Money class said to me, "I've watched the way you always use the things that happen in your life—even bad stuff—to your advantage. I had to see you being that before I started doing it for myself. It's quite amazing what shows up when you don't judge your choices and you allow them to contribute to you, even if in the moment something didn't turn out all that great."

I said, "Well, what makes you think something didn't turn out all that great? Maybe it's greater than you know. Every time I think something is not working, I am surprised to find out what does work."

Everything is possible if you don't see something as a problem. The moment you define something as a problem, you take away the possibility. When something weird goes on, when someone cheats you or deceives you and you find out you owe a ton of money you didn't know you owed, how do you deal with it? Everything is possible if you don't see something as a problem. The moment you define something as a problem, you take away the possibility. What are you creating? Loss of finances? Loss of money? Loss of life? Or all of the above and more?

What have you made so vital, valuable and real about the inevitability of the loss of finances through death that keeps you looking for the reasons and justifications for creating poverty? Everything that is times a godzillion, will you destroy and uncreate it all? Right and Wrong, Good and Bad, POD and POC, All 9, Shorts, Boys, and Beyonds.

Look for the Infinite Possibility

I live in Texas where people own oil wells. At one point I was with a bunch of people who were talking about their oil wells, and I thought, "Where's my oil well, so I can get millions of dollars?" Then I said, "Oh! If I'm going to have an oil well, I have to at least own land where they can drill for oil. I don't have that." That was pretty funny. I was being like people who ask, "Where's all my money? I want to win the lottery." Well, if you are going to win the lottery, you must consider the possibility of actually playing the lottery!

If you want money, you've got to acknowledge, "I'm good at creating not enough." Then you've got to ask: "What would it be like if I was creating too much? What is really true here? What do I really want? What am I really creating? What is the item for me that is going to make everything greater?"

It's not: "How do I get this right?" or "Why don't I have lots of money?" It's not about the thing you see as a solution. If you see the lottery as your solution to not having enough money, you are not going to get what you want. Why? Because you have decided there is only one path. The great thing about being enthusiastic is that you have multiple paths, and each one creates a different sense of lightness and a different set of possibilities. You don't see one path as the answer.

Most people look for the answer—not the infinite possibility. Start looking for the infinite possibility! The more happy, joyful, creative, and enthusiastic you are for what can occur, the more the road to the success and money you desire will show up.

I have some friends who were looking for property in Australia. They made an offer on a property; the owner accepted their offer and then later backed out. They said, "Oh no! What are we going to do?"

I said, "Look for another property. What? Is this the only property in the world?"

They said, "But this one was so great!"

I asked, "What if you went out and found something even greater? The universe has your back and it wants to create more for you if you have the enthusiasm, if you have the willingness and the ability to create, and if you are willing to look at what else you can add to your life and how you can create more. You have to start looking from the creation of, not the solution to the problem of."

A lady recently sent me ten questions asking how to get out of her problem. It was all about the limitation of this and the limitation of that. It was about how she doesn't have—and not about how she has. Most people are looking at how to get out of their problems instead of how to create beyond. Do you look at what you have? And are you grateful for it?

I have filled my house with antiques so I can walk around being grateful for having such beautiful things in my life. Every day I walk in my house and say, "Wow! How did I get to be so lucky to have this? To live like this? To have a life in which this is what I get to be and have and do?" I wake up in the morning saying, "I am so grateful. How lucky am I? How the hell did I get so lucky to have this as my life? What did I do?"

I did not do all the things that people say get you the best in life. For a long time, drugs, sex, and rock-and-roll was my way of life, but I always had an enthusiasm for living. You've got to have an enthusiasm for living.

> How much of your enthusiasm for living are you suppressing so you never have to live from the total enthusiasm of living? Everything that is times a godzillion, will you destroy and uncreate it all? Right and Wrong, Good and Bad, POD and POC, All 9, Shorts, Boys, and Beyonds.

Please do the following questions again—and then again. And choose to live from the joy of creation, the joy of choice, and the joy of possibility.

WORKBOOK QUESTIONS
CHAPTER SEVEN

QUESTION ONE: *What enthusiasm can I be to create a totally different reality for me?*

_____

_____

_____

_____

_____

QUESTION TWO: *Where have I bought that my life has to be miserable instead of enthusiastic?*

_____

_____

_____

_____

_____

QUESTION THREE: *What have I done to make myself a refusenik today?*

_____

_____

_____

_____

_____

CHAPTER EIGHT

MONEY IS EASY

Here is your first question. Please write down your answers.

QUESTION ONE: *If I was having everything I desire in life, what would I have to be?*

_____

_____

_____

_____

_____

What have you made so vital, valuable, and real about the inevitability of being what you have to be in order to get what you truly desire that you refuse to be in order not to get what you truly desire? Do you see how silly this is? Do you get that you are working against yourself? Why are you your own worst enemy? You are fighting against everything you say you desire and everything you say you want. Good choice? Bad choice? Incredible stupidity? Everything that is times a godzillion, will you destroy and uncreate it all? Right and Wrong, Good and Bad, POD and POC, All 9, Shorts, Boys, and Beyonds.

QUESTION TWO: *Where and when did I decide that I was the only one who was smart enough to stop me from getting everything I truly desire?*

_____

_____

_____

_____

Where and when did you decide that you were the only one who was smart enough to get everything that you truly desire so you wouldn't get everything you truly desire? Everything that is times a godzillion, will you destroy and uncreate it all? Right and Wrong, Good and Bad, POD and POC, All 9, Shorts, Boys, and Beyonds.

Making the Demand

This is where you have to make the demand: "I don't know what the hell I am doing, but obviously I am not getting what I truly desire, so whatever it takes to change this, I am changing it." You have to make that kind of demand.

You also have to recognize that you have created people in your life who can do a whole lot of things, and they will assist you in what you wish to create. Today I was talking with a friend who found out that her father let 950 cattle go totally wild because he wasn't willing to make the cowboys go out and do their job. She said, "I don't know how we are going to collect these cows."

I called a kid I met at the Conscious Horse, Conscious Rider class and I asked, "Do you know anyone who could collect these cows?"

He called back in five minutes and said, "I've got people ready to do that." Say what? This is the way it works. When you're willing to ask the questions: "What's it going to take to create this?" and "What's it going to take to create a different possibility?" the universe will do everything it can to support you—if you do not refuse to be it and to have it.

There is possibility in the world that few people are able to see. Who's capable of seeing it? Anybody who chooses to. But you choose not to. Why do you choose not to? I am trying to get you to choose. There's so much available to you, and you are acting like you have no choice.

Affluence or Effluence?

Do you get that you are not choosing affluence? You may have misidentified and misapplied effluence and affluence. Effluence is when you have diarrhea. Affluence is when you have too much money. Someone told me she looked up those words in a dictionary from 1828. She said, "Effluence is a flowing out or forth. Affluence is a flowing towards. It's an abundance of riches. I love that effluence is flowing out and affluence is flowing to."

What would it be like if you were willing to recognize that affluence was a state of receiving that you have been refusing? Everything that doesn't allow you to have that level of receiving, will you destroy and uncreate it all? Right and Wrong, Good and Bad, POD and POC, All 9, Shorts, Boys, and Beyonds.

You may have changed enough to know that's true, yet you still refuse to change the money situation in your life. You could give that up, but you probably won't. You think poverty is way more fun than affluence.

Where and when did you decide that you were the only one who was smart enough to stop you from getting everything you truly desire? Everything that is times a godzillion, will you destroy and uncreate it all? Right and Wrong, Good and Bad, POD and POC, All 9, Shorts, Boys, and Beyonds.

What have you made so vital, valuable, and real about poverty that keeps you from choosing that which would create affluence? Most of you think affluence is like effluence, or having a fart. Affluence is not having a fart. It's creating money.

This is the reason I ask you to look up words in the dictionary. If you look up words, you begin to see what they really mean and you get to choose a different reality. If you don't look them up and you don't know what they mean, do you have a real awareness of what is available to you? No.

Would you get that one of the ways you refuse affluence, abundance, and having too much money is by not educating yourself on what you are saying and thinking? Everything you have done to not have total awareness of what you are saying and thinking, will you destroy and uncreate all that? Right and Wrong, Good and Bad, POD and POC, All 9, Shorts, Boys, and Beyonds.

What energy, space, and consciousness are you using to avoid the awareness and the education that would give you the affluence are you choosing? Everything that is times a godzillion, will you destroy and uncreate it all? Right and Wrong, Good and Bad, POD and POC, All 9, Shorts, Boys, and Beyonds.

Educate Yourself About What You Are Saying and Thinking

A lady told me, "I just looked up the word receive because receiving is something I have had difficulty with. The first meaning is 'to be given, presented with, or paid.' The second meaning is 'to suffer, experience, or be subject to.' I get that I've taken on the second meaning."

This is what many of you have done. You've taken the meaning of words that justify the limitations you are creating.

> Everything you have done to avoid educating yourself on how to get more and be more, and everything you have done to educate yourself on how to limit yourself more, will you destroy and uncreate all that? Right and Wrong, Good and Bad, POD and POC, All 9, Shorts, Boys, and Beyonds.

> What have you made so vital, valuable, and real about poverty that keeps you from choosing that which would create affluence? Everything that is times a godzillion, will you destroy and uncreate it all? Right and Wrong, Good and Bad, POD and POC, All 9, Shorts, Boys, and Beyonds.

What do you really want to create in your life? Do you want to create more money than you ever thought was possible? Or have you already decided you can't have it?

Have you made yourself totally depressed about what you have decided you can't have because you obviously can't have it because you don't have it? Will you destroy and uncreate all that? Right and Wrong, Good and Bad, POD and POC, All 9, Shorts, Boys, and Beyonds.

QUESTION THREE: *What enthusiasm am I avoiding to make sure I don't succeed financially?*

_____

_____

_____

_____

_____

Demand Allows You to Choose Enthusiasm

There's a difference between having enthusiasm and being enthusiasm. If you have enthusiasm, you are lying. If you are being enthusiasm, you have no point of view; you are just enjoying the hell out of yourself. When you are enthusiasm, you continue to do things no matter what occurs. You don't stop your life and you don't stop yourself. You look for greater possibility. What would happen if you looked for greater possibilities always?

Demand is what allows you to choose enthusiasm. You have to demand of yourself, "I'm going to create a greater life than anybody else is willing to have."

I'm willing to create what nobody else is willing to have, and I don't care what I get. I just enjoy everything I receive. I am enthusiastic about the fact that I have a capacity to perceive, know, be, and receive greater than other people are willing to perceive, know, be, or receive. Why is that true? Because that is what creates possibility and joy and everything else.

You are grateful for what you have and you are grateful for what's going on. Gratitude and enthusiasm go hand in hand. They are like the yin and the yang of possibility. You have to create a demand. You have to ask: "What do I really want to create and how do I do this?"

Just Choose

A class participant said, "Sometimes I ask, 'What would I like to create?' and I don't necessarily know how to create it..."

I said, "'How do I create it?' is a not a question that opens the door to possibility. Ask: 'What would I have to choose here that would create this?'"

She said, "I ask that, and then I don't have an answer."

I said, "That's because there is no answer to what you have to choose. There is only the possibility of what you can choose. So you just choose."

She said, "Oh! That's what you said the other day: 'Just choose.' I get it now!"

If I'm Not Enjoying This, Why the Hell Am I Here?

Another class participant asked, "Gary, have you always been that enthusiasm?"

I said, "Yeah, I've always had an enthusiasm for life because I thought, 'If I'm not enjoying this, or I'm not enthusiastic, why the hell am I here?'"

She said, "When I returned from the seven-day event in South Africa, I had that sort of enthusiasm. It's there again now, but for a while it was all gone. What's that?"

I said, "It wasn't gone. It's just that nobody could receive it. You have the idea that if somebody can't receive something, you have to quit having it. I don't have that point of view. I am enthusiastic whether anybody else likes it or not."

She said, "Yes! I was buying into this reality. It's like there is no joy there. Most people don't have joy."

Most people are not willing to have the enthusiasm and the creativity that would allow for their lives because they would go beyond everybody they know.

QUESTION FOUR: *Who or what am I unwilling to go beyond that if I went beyond them would create a totally different financial reality for me?*

_____

_____

_____

_____

_____

Don't Give Up Your Reality

Once when I was younger, my mother came to visit me in Santa Barbara. She said, "I'll take you out to dinner, honey. Where do you want to go?"

I said, "How about the Ranch House in Ojai?"

She said, "That sounds fine."

We went there and the cost of the dinner for three of us was $120. She paid it and then she asked, "Why would you ever eat at this restaurant?" The Ranch House has some of the best food you will ever eat in your life, but three people having a dinner that cost $120 was horrifying for her. I looked at that and thought, "Okay, my mum and I don't have the same reality." I didn't go to "She's wrong." I didn't go to "I'm wrong." It was "We don't have the same reality."

I realized, "I can't do this to her again," and I never did. Later on when I had money and my mother and my stepdad came to visit, I took them to a really nice restaurant, and I paid. This time my stepdad was the one who was horrified—because it was a gourmet restaurant and he wanted a hamburger. The staff had to do extra work to find a way to get the man a hamburger. His point of view was "Why would you spend this kind of money to get such a bad hamburger?" At that point, I got that my reality and their reality would never meet.

My stepdad wanted to go across the street where he could have "all you can eat" for $7.99. That's not my reality. I wasn't willing to give up my reality but I was very happy to take him to the $7.99 place and drink while he ate.

Have I ever given up my reality for anyone else? Yes, I did it with my wives. I spent my entire time being married trying to give up my reality to make them happy. But can you really make anybody else happy? No.

QUESTION FIVE: *How much of my reality have I given up to make other people happy which has never succeeded?*

_____

_____

_____

_____

_____

You eliminate your choices when you give up your own reality.

Someone in a class said, "I would like unlimited choice."

I said, "You can't have it. I won't let you."

She laughed and said, "Keep telling me that." She knew that my saying she couldn't have unlimited choice was exactly what it would take to get her to make the demand to have it.

I said, "Notice that when I said, 'You can't have it,' in your head, you said, 'No one is ever going to hold me down again!' That's a decision you have to make."

QUESTION SIX: *What decision would I have to make today that would create my financial reality right away?*

_____

_____

_____

_____

_____

What decision would you have to make based on the fact that you tend to make decisions that stop you instead of moving you to create? The question is basically tricking yourself into moving beyond the ridiculous decisions you have made. You would rather make a decision that makes you a pile of shit than one that makes you an unlimited being with unlimited capacity.

A lady who is an artist said, "When I am creating a picture or a painting, I am in the moment, but when I am creating my life, I make all sorts of decisions and conclusions."

I said, "When you are creating a picture, you have to stay in the moment or it doesn't actualize as something worth having, does it? The same thing applies to your life."

Money Is Everywhere

The first *How to Become Money Workbook* asks the question, "When you see money coming toward you, from which direction do you see it coming?" Some people see money coming at them from behind, others from the left or the right or from above them. You have to have the point of view that money is everywhere and it is everything. You ask: "How is money going to work for me?"

You are always looking at how you can create money. You are not looking at what money is going to create for you. If money was going to work for you, what would that look like? What would it look like if every dollar you spent was going to come back to you tenfold? What would it be like if every time you spent money, something great would occur for you?

QUESTION SEVEN: *How is money going to work for me?*

_____

_____

_____

_____

_____

I have a friend who spent a lot of money getting her land cleared of bad weeds and garbage. She said, "The energy from the land is amazing."

I asked, "When you buy a really nice dress, do you feel better when you are in it?"

She said, "Totally."

I said, "So when you are about to spend money, ask: 'How does this make me feel? Does this expand my life or does this contract my life?'"

How do you create with money? How is money going to work for you? You've got to have money working for you. You are of the opinion that you must always work to get your money. Too many people are in the musical work mode, "I owe, I owe, so off to work I go."

I'm not talking about investing and receiving from what you invest in. Investing is the point of view that you only have a certain amount and if you invest that, it must return an amount that makes doing the investment worthwhile. That is all judgment! Getting money to work for you is completely different.

The question is: "How is this money going to work for me?" That's the question! "How is it going to work for me?"

Money Is Easy

You don't want to know that money is that easy, because if money were that easy, what the hell would you do? You'd have to give up your hard life. I want you to be able to demand what you desire in life and be willing to have it. Does what you desire always show up instantaneously? No. But it will show up. What is it going to look like? I don't know. When is it going to show up? I don't know. You've just got to be willing to look at it from a different place.

A friend recently went to her first auction. She said she had a sense of bubbling joy, just being there. Looking at all the beautiful things that were being sold, she realized she was not anywhere near choosing furniture or other items for herself that made her feel light and expansive.

She said, "I saw a mirror and my whole body went 'ahhhh.' It sold for $5,000. Because I've been listening to you about antiques, I did a little bit of research on it. I found out it was called a Pier 1760 mirror. One of them sold at Christie's for $55,000."

I asked, "You mean you knew something when you looked at the mirror?"

She said, "Yeah, what is that when you deny your knowing instantaneously?"

I said, "Well, I'm sorry. If you knew what you know all the time—and you could make money that easily—that would make your life too easy, and you cannot have an easy life."

She said, "Well, I'm done with that! I've noticed that if I have a bit of time off, instead of receiving the time and the beauty of creation and the joy, there's an automatic responder to go to shit around money rather than just being and receiving of life."

I said, "Well, that's because you make money more important than receiving. That's not a good idea, is it?"

Educate Yourself About What You Love

Educate yourself about that which is going to make you money. What are you interested in? What do you love? What makes your heart sing? I love antiques. I look at antiques everywhere I go. When I see something super beautiful I ask, "How much is that?" If I can't afford it, I can't afford it. The next time I see something that's equally beautiful in a price range I can afford, I buy it.

I also look at what other people don't see. Money comes to those who see what other people cannot see, or what they don't want to see, or what they have points of view about. I once went to a garage sale run by an older lady. I saw a fourteen-carat gold bracelet that was marked $1500. I thought, "I wonder how much this actually is. Is she asking $150 or $1500?" Two antique dealers had left the sale in front of me without showing any interest in it.

I asked the lady, "How much is this?"

She said, "It's $15 and it's fourteen-carat gold," so I bought it. That afternoon I went to a store that buys gold and silver items and sold it for $450. Everybody said, "How can you take advantage of that little old lady?"

I said, "It's easy. I paid her exactly what she asked."

QUESTION EIGHT: *If I was totally willing to receive, what would I end up being?*

_____

_____

_____

_____

_____

You ask for more money and the universe says, "Okay, here's more money," and it shows you something like a $5,000 mirror or a $15 bracelet, and you say, "No." Why do you say "No"? Why don't you ask, "What is it going to take for me to create this?" You don't have to buy everything that comes your way. Research the thing and find out what it's worth. The next time you see something that is worth a lot of money, you'll say, "Everything in me tells me this is worth a lot of money. How can I buy it?" and then buy it.

There's an auction site here in the United States that I sometimes go onto. I hadn't done it for many months, and for some reason, I went on it recently. I bought a bunch of loose stones, which I paid basically nothing for, that nobody seems to want. Does that make me sad? No. I bid the amount I wanted to bid and I said, "If I 'lose' on them, I don't care because I don't believe it's a loss. I believe it is an opening to a door of a different possibility. What would be available if I didn't have a fixed point of view?" That's the next question:

QUESTION NINE: *What would be available if I had no fixed points of view?*

_____

_____

_____

_____

_____

You could have everything if you would eliminate your points of view, but you would rather have your points of view because that proves that you are you.

What have you made so vital, real, and valuable about your points of view that keep you inevitably choosing against what would create money and possibility in your life, as you? Everything that is times a godzillion, will you destroy and uncreate it all? Right and Wrong, Good and Bad, POD and POC, All 9, Shorts, Boys, and Beyonds.

What have you made so vital, valuable, and real about the inevitability of being a pauper on the street that keeps you from creating that which would make you a millionaire on top of the mountain? Everything that is times a godzillion, will you destroy and uncreate it all? Right and Wrong, Good and Bad, POD and POC, All 9, Shorts, Boys, and Beyonds.

Please remember that money is easy. And please work with these questions over and over again so you become aware of your limitations around money and you no longer buy them as true.

WORKBOOK QUESTIONS
CHAPTER EIGHT

QUESTION ONE: *If I was having everything I desire in life, what would I have to be?*

_____

_____

_____

_____

_____

QUESTION TWO: *Where and when did I decide that I was the only one who was smart enough to stop me from getting everything I truly desire?*

_____

_____

_____

_____

_____

QUESTION THREE: *What enthusiasm am I avoiding to make sure I don't succeed financially?*

_____

_____

_____

_____

_____

QUESTION FOUR: *Who or what am I unwilling to go beyond that if I went beyond them would create a totally different financial reality for me?*

_____
_____
_____
_____
_____

QUESTION FIVE: *How much of my reality have I given up to make other people happy which has never succeeded?*

_____
_____
_____
_____
_____

QUESTION SIX: *What decision would I have to make today that would create my financial reality right away?*

_____
_____
_____
_____

QUESTION SEVEN: *How is money going to work for me?*

_____
_____
_____
_____

QUESTION EIGHT: *If I was totally willing to receive, what would I end up being?*

_____

_____

_____

_____

_____

QUESTION NINE: *What would be available if I had no fixed points of view?*

_____

_____

_____

_____

_____

CHAPTER NINE

A FUTURE BEYOND ANYTHING YOU HAVE EVER SEEN

QUESTION ONE: *What have I defined as my last resort when I am out of money?*

_____

_____

_____

_____

_____

You may have decided that your last resort is to be homeless, or your last resort is to go live with your mum, or your last resort is to get married. Whatever it is that you have defined as your last resort becomes the thing you seek when you are not seeking creation. When you are creating your last resort, you are not creating your life.

What have you concluded is your last resort if you are out of money that keeps you creating for the last resort? Everything that is times a godzillion, will you destroy and uncreate it all? Right and Wrong, Good and Bad, POD and POC, All 9, Shorts, Boys, and Beyonds.

We must always seek the last resort if we are not seeking creation.

Everything you have done to not seek the creation, will you destroy and uncreate all that? Right and Wrong, Good and Bad, POD and POC, All 9, Shorts, Boys, and Beyonds.

Whatever you come up with as your last resort, you've got to ask: "Is this really my last resort? Or do I have something available I've never even considered?" That's the next question:

QUESTION TWO: *If this is my last resort, what is it that I have never considered?*

_____

_____

_____

_____

_____

When you are willing to consider anything as a possibility, you can come out of "I have no choice" and move into "What choices do I have?" You can also ask: "If I chose something different, what would I have to be or do to create that?" That's question number three:

QUESTION THREE: *If I chose something different, what would I have to be or do to create that?*

_____

_____

_____

_____

_____

There's always a different possibility. You always have a choice. And every choice creates something. Even "no choice" is a choice you make, and it creates something.

> How many no choices have you made in your life which limit the money you can have? Everything that is times a godzillion, will you destroy and uncreate it all? Right and Wrong, Good and Bad, POD and POC, All 9, Shorts, Boys, and Beyonds.

> What is actually possible that you haven't considered? What if you chose something different? What would you have to be or do to create that? Everything that doesn't allow that times a godzillion, will you destroy and uncreate it all? Right and Wrong, Good and Bad, POD and POC, All 9, Shorts, Boys, and Beyonds.

Possibilities come up even when you choose no choice. If you choose no choice, you go to the last resort. You say, "If all else fails, I would have to choose...." What?

What choice did you make when you decided you had no choice? Everything that is times a godzillion, will you destroy and uncreate it all? Right and Wrong, Good and Bad, POD and POC, All 9, Shorts, Boys, and Beyonds.

If all else fails, what would you have to choose? Everything that is times a godzillion, will you destroy and uncreate it all? Right and Wrong, Good and Bad, POD and POC, All 9, Shorts, Boys, and Beyonds.

A lady asked me about a person she was facilitating. She said, "He has a high-profile job that creates a lot of money. He's about to jump off a cliff, and he knows that his point of view about money is sticking him."

Is your point of view about money sticking you? You have to look at what you're doing and ask, "What is this? What can I do with it? What do I want to choose here? What would actually work for me if I chose it?" Choose to recognize what is and then you can ask a question like: "What are the choices possible here?"

What have you made so valuable, vital, real, and valid about money that creates the inevitability of never having unlimited amounts? Everything that is times a godzillion, will you destroy and uncreate it all? Right and Wrong, Good and Bad, POD and POC, All 9, Shorts, Boys, and Beyonds.

You've Got to Create Your Future

People often want to talk with me about things that happened in the past. I ask, "Why are you making that real? Why are you looking at the past instead of creating your future?" The problem lies in you—not in your past. Your past did not create what you are doing today; you did. You use your past as a justification, but the past is not a reality. It's a choice you make that keeps the past more relevant than your future.

What would you have to be, do, have, create, and generate as your future to annihilate and eradicate all relevance of past for all eternity? Everything that is times a godzillion, will you destroy and uncreate it all? Right and Wrong, Good and Bad, POD and POC, All 9, Shorts, Boys, and Beyonds.

You keep looking to the past as though that's the gift. The past is not the gift. The past is the past. What do you want to create? More of the past? Less of the past? Or do you want a future that is beyond anything you have ever seen?

What would you have to be, do, have, create, and generate as your future to annihilate and eradicate all relevance of the past for all eternity? If you see that choice creates, why the hell are you not creating? What choice would you have to make right now to create a different reality financially?

I had a conversation with a friend who said, "We've got a ton of taxes to pay that we haven't planned for. We are also looking at buying an investment property. Part of me wants to say, 'Let's get everything flourishing, let's get the tax paid, let's get all this done, and then invest in the property.' Another part wants to say, 'Let's just create and choose it all,' but I don't wish to get into a financial mess. I'm unsure about what choices to make."

I said, "Let's look at it from a slightly different point of view. As you know, I've been looking at the possibility of buying a ranch so I can bring my horses to Texas because they are costing so much in California. I can probably reduce my outflow significantly by buying a ranch here."

My friend said, "That choice is a no-brainer. I would choose that. In buying the ranch, you are creating a future that's going to be far larger in five, ten, fifteen, or twenty years, and I know that you can create more."

I said, "Exactly. Years ago when the state of California confiscated all my cash for taxes, I went to Bonhams and spent $31,000 on jewelry for the Antique Guild. You and everybody who was with me said, 'How can you do that when you owe so much in taxes?'"

I said, "Hey, I just owe taxes. I'm not dead. I'm going to create my future. You've got to create your future. You can look at your tax bill and say, 'Okay, I owe all this tax money. Now what? These are the ways I can pay it: I can sell everything I own and pay off the taxes. Is that going to be creating my life or destroying my life? Destroying it.' Or you can ask: 'If I'm going to create my life, what is it going to look like? What is it going to look like if I do this?'"

My friend said, "The property we'd like to buy is going to auction next month. It's probably going to be $500,000. We are looking at knocking down the house that's on the land and building three townhouses on it. That's probably going to be around $1.1 million. We keep laughing about how we are not going small with our investment. We are going big. Why would we go small?"

I said, "Unfortunately, you've been doing Access too long."

She laughed and said, "Sometimes this reality starts to pull you back and say, 'Hey, you have over $100,000 in taxes to pay. You need to cut back.' That's not my world; that's not my reality. I've never cut back. I create more."

I said, "You have to look at what creates the enthusiasm in your life. Paying the government? Or creating something for you? If you're doing something that is a little bit above your comfort level and you're asking, 'How is this going to work?' look at what the worst-case scenario is. Could you rent out your house for more than you are paying on it and rent another house for less than what you are paying now? That money could go for paying off your taxes. You have choices. We tend to buy the idea that we have no choices rather than looking at what is actually possible. You have different sources for money.

"Create choices in life, and that will create more. I always want to function from what's going to create more in my life. Don't function from the last resort, 'I have to pay all my taxes and die.' Look at what creates the enthusiasm in your life. Paying the government? Or creating something for you? What do you want to create in your life? What's really important to you?"

The Point of View One Takes Determines the Creation One Has and Gets

At one point, I looked at giving away all my horses because that would reduce my monthly outflow by over $20,000 a month. Should I actually have just given them away? No. I brought this breed to the United States because of a long-term reality, which is our center in Costa Rica, which should be up and running within two years. There will be people from Costa Rica, the United States, Europe, and all around the world riding these horses. They are going to want one. Why? Because they are wonderful horses. They are amazing horses. Once you've ridden one, you ask, "How do I find one?" Well, I just happen to have a place where we breed them. So I am planning long term; I am not planning short term.

Most businesses fail in the first two years, and the reason for the failure is lack of sufficient money to run them in the first place. You've got to have resources to be able to start a business. Is that always necessary? Well, no, but you can't expect to make massive amounts of money in the first year or two. By the third year you can start to make money and by the fourth year you can make really good money.

Someone said, "I would shut down if I had to pay a huge tax bill. How can you function like that?"

I said, "It's just a tax bill. It's not the end of the world. Am I going to die? No. Are they going to take me away to debtors prison? No. They can't even send me to Australia anymore." The point of view that one takes determines the creation one has and gets. Am I saying, "Oh my God! This is terrible. Taxes!" No! What would I be creating with that point of view? Possibility? Or dread? Which one creates your future?"

QUESTION FOUR: *If I was creating my future, what would I choose and how would I know what to choose?*

_____

_____

_____

_____

_____

_____

QUESTION FIVE: *How can I create more than I've ever had before?*

_____

_____

_____

_____

_____

_____

Judgment vs. Interesting Point of View

Whenever you are doing any kind of judgment, even of you, you are eliminating consciousness as a reality. If you really desire consciousness, you have to get rid of all judgment. Consciousness includes everything and judges nothing. You have to be willing to receive anything without a point of view. You have to see it as a possibility and what it will create by what you choose.

Sometimes people come to me and say, "I have to talk to you. Do you know what I do for money? I grow pot."

I say, "Okay, fine. There's a market for everything in the world." They are looking for my judgment. It's about who they get to reject and who they don't have to receive. If I say,

"It's terrible that you do that," they can reject me and everything I've told them that could create more for them. But I'm interested in creating more for them, not less.

You have to function from Interesting Point of View. Everything is just an interesting point of view. Interesting Point of View is a choice you have. Your point of view simply creates possibilities. Are you using it? Or are you avoiding it?

There are ways to make money everywhere in the world. You just have to find what you are interested in, what is fun for you, and what can make money for you. Are you doing that? Or are you trying to work at the right thing to make sure you get the right money? Here's the next thing for you to do:

QUESTION SIX: *What ten things have I decided are "wrong money"?*

_____

_____

_____

_____

_____

QUESTION SEVEN: *What are ten things have I decided are "right money"?*

_____

_____

_____

_____

_____

Now look at each thing you've written down and ask: "Is that a judgment about what's right money and wrong money?"

> What have you defined as right money that keeps you from having money? Everything that is times a godzillion, will you destroy and uncreate it all? Right and Wrong, Good and Bad, POD and POC, All 9, Shorts, Boys, and Beyonds.

> What have you decided and determined as wrong money that keeps you from having money? Everything that is times a godzillion, will you destroy

and uncreate it all? Right and Wrong, Good and Bad, POD and POC, All 9, Shorts, Boys, and Beyonds.

When you decide something has to be or can't be, are you really at choice?

If You're Not Willing to Be Something, You Can't Receive Anything

Sometimes people who become Access facilitators tell me, "I'm not making any money." What question is that? They never ask, "Why am I not making enough money?" because the answer to that one is "You are not making enough money because there is something you are not willing to be." If you're not willing to be something, you can't receive anything. You have got to be willing to be everything in order to receive everything. That's why I've written this workbook: If you can become money, you can receive money and have money. But you have to be willing to be whatever it takes to create the money you desire.

QUESTION EIGHT: *What would I have to be to create the money I would like to receive?*

_____

_____

_____

_____

_____

Whatever you decide you can't be keeps you from having the money you desire. You've got to be willing to be it in order to have it.

"How Can I Use My Money to Create Money?"

Are you getting this? You may have to read this book more than once or twice. This is the advanced book. Most people can't even do basic money. Why can't they do basic money? Because they are more interested in how they can spend their money than how they can use their money to create greater possibility. You've got to ask: "How can I use my money?"

I've gone to swap meets when I only had $10—and I've bought things that were worth $20 or $50. If you've only got $10 and you are going to spend it, don't buy a cup of coffee. Buy something that is worth more than you are paying for it. Ask: "How can I use my money to create money?"

Don't listen to people who say, "You've got to use other people's money to make money" or "You've got to take advantage of others in order to get the money you want" or "Money is bad." Money is not inherently right or wrong or good or bad. It just is. What is it? It is what it is! It doesn't mean anything until you make it meaningful.

I started taking my kids to garage sales when they were very young. I'd have them buy stuff and then I'd sell it for them so they would learn there is a place where they can always go to get money. Most of them now have the point of view "Okay, what can I do that is going to make the most money for me?" because I gave them the skills that would allow them to make a reasonable income with little to no money to start with.

Someone told me, "My son's point of view is 'Of course I have money. Of course there's money.'"

I said, "That's a good thing. That gives him the point of view that money is not hard to come by. If his point of view is 'Of course there's money,' then he can ask, 'What do I have to do to get it?'"

I've had friends who grew up with money and I noticed something about them. They never used the words why, try, want, and need. Those words didn't exist in their vocabulary. They had the point of view "Of course I will have money." When they got married, they married someone who had money. They didn't marry a poor person who struggled.

They happened to have parents who had bought property in Newport Beach when it was cheap, so they had money and they were always going to have money. They were going to be millionaires simply by inheritance alone. They expected money to be part of their lives. They had no expectation that they couldn't have it. I taught my kids they could have money too, and there was always a way to get it if they were willing to do it.

My parents had the point of view that you had to work hard and save your money. So they worked hard, they saved their money, and they had nothing. They passed up every possibility they had to make money. In 1942 they had a chance to buy a square block for $600 in a little California beach town called La Jolla. They didn't buy it because my mother's point of view was that you should save your money, not invest it. La Jolla is now a very hot property.

When I was thirteen, my parents had a chance to buy a 100-acre farm in a place called El Cajon for the same price as a 1,400-square-foot tract house. They chose to buy the tract house. It was brand new, and they thought it was really cool. Two years later, the freeway went through the farm land and the farmer who owned it got a million dollars. The world will give you possibilities for creating money if you are willing to look for the possibilities of what creates money.

I started out with nothing because that was my family's point of view. I created money out of nothing. People say, "You have nothing when you come in and you'll have nothing when you go out." I say, "Bullshit! That's not my reality."

You can create something out of nothing because you are the something that will never have nothing. If your family poisons the well in terms of what you're able to create, don't drink. If they poison the pie, don't eat. What are you trying to buy of your family's reality that is not yours? You have to ask, "What's my reality?" Is your family's reality that they're going to create lots of money? No? Why is that? Because for them, lack is real. But is lack real in your reality?

When I had no money, I wanted to buy a house, and I found a way to buy one with no money down. As I was looking for a property to buy, I said, "Universe, show me where I can buy a property that is going to be worth a lot more."

It turned out that the house was in a "bad area," but it was a no-money-down deal. The people wanted to get rid of the property so badly that they were willing to do anything to sell it. You've got to be willing to look at what can be created, not assume that something cannot get created.

QUESTION NINE: *What possibilities for having money am I not choosing?*

Questions Create

Many years ago a lady came after me. She wanted to marry me. She was married at the time I met her, and I wouldn't have anything to do with her because I didn't go out with married women. I went to Europe for six months. When I came back, she started going after me again, but I just put her off and never asked anybody if she was still married. Oops. Questions create. It turned out she'd gotten a divorce. Six months after that she married a man who looked enough like me to be my brother. After another six months, she died of a cerebral hemorrhage from birth control pills and left him $67 million. Possibilities show up in our lives, but we don't always take them. Unfortunately, if we don't ask a question, we can't receive.

"What's My Reality?"

I was talking with my friend who wanted to buy a piece of property and build townhouses on it. She said, "Buying this property feels like fun to me. I've been asking, 'Will this make me happy? Will I learn something? Will this be fun for me?' Then I realized those are the same questions we ask about having sex with someone!"

I said, "Yeah, because sex and money go hand in hand." They're both about receiving. I have been trying to give this information away my whole life.

The fact that you are willing to hear what I have to say is an indication that you are a humanoid. Your reality is not like other people's and you will not have a disaster-zone reality. That is not your reality. It has never been your reality. Your reality has always been about having more in life. Please recognize this. You are not willing to live your life with less. You are willing to live your life for more.

This is something I know about every person who comes to Access. They are looking for the more that they always knew was their reality. You cannot fail if you are willing to create the more that you are.

I will be grateful to you if you make a ton of money. You want to pay me back? Make a bunch of money! And please do the following questions again—and then again.

WORKBOOK QUESTIONS
CHAPTER NINE

QUESTION ONE: *What have I defined as my last resort when I am out of money?*

_____

_____

_____

_____

QUESTION TWO: *If this is my last resort, what is it that I have never considered?*

_____

_____

_____

_____

QUESTION THREE: *If I chose something different, what would I have to be or do to create that?*

_____

_____

_____

_____

QUESTION FOUR: *If I was creating my future, what would I choose and how would I know what to choose?*

_____

_____

_____

_____

_____

QUESTION FIVE: *How can I create more than I've ever had before?*

_____

_____

_____

_____

_____

QUESTION SIX: *What ten things have I decided are "wrong money"? Look at each thing you've written down and ask: "Is that a judgment about what's wrong money?"*

_____

_____

_____

_____

_____

QUESTION SEVEN: *What are ten things I have decided are "right money"? Look at each thing you've written down and ask: "Is that a judgment about what's right money?"*

_____

_____

_____

_____

_____

QUESTION EIGHT: *What would I have to be to create the money I would like to receive?*

_____

_____

_____

_____

_____

QUESTION NINE: *What possibilities for having money am I not choosing?*

_____

_____

_____

_____

_____

THE ACCESS CONSCIOUSNESS CLEARING STATEMENT®

You are the only one who can unlock the points
of view that have you trapped.
What I am offering here with the clearing process is a tool
you can use to change the energy of the points of view
that have you locked into unchanging situations.

Throughout this book, I ask a lot of questions, and some of these questions might twist your head around a little bit. That's my intention. The questions I ask are designed to get your mind out of the picture so you can get to the energy of a situation.

Once the question has twisted your head around and brought up the energy of a situation, I ask if you are willing to destroy and uncreate that energy—because stuck energy is the source of barriers and limitations. Destroying and uncreating that energy will open the door to new possibilities for you.

This is your opportunity to say, "Yes, I'm willing to let go of whatever is holding that limitation in place."

That will be followed by some weird-speak we call the clearing statement:

Right and Wrong, Good and Bad, POD and POC, All 9, Shorts, Boys, and Beyonds.

With the clearing statement, we're going back to the energy of the limitations and barriers that have been created. We're looking at the energies that keep us from moving forward and expanding into all of the spaces that we would like to go. The clearing statement is simply short-speak that addresses the energies that are creating the limitations and contractions in our life.

The more you run the clearing statement, the deeper it goes and the more layers and levels it can unlock for you. If a lot of energy comes up for you in response to a question, you may wish to repeat the process numerous times until the subject being addressed is no longer an issue for you.

You don't have to understand the words of the clearing statement for it to work because it's about the energy. However, if you're interested in knowing what the words mean, some brief definitions are given below.

Right and Wrong, Good and Bad is shorthand for: What's right, good, perfect, and correct about this? What's wrong, mean, vicious, terrible, bad, and awful about this? The short version of these questions is: What's right and wrong, good and bad? It is the things that we consider right, good, perfect, and/or correct that stick us the most. We do not wish to let go of them since we decided that we have them right.

POD stands for the point of destruction; all the ways you have been destroying yourself in order to keep whatever you're clearing in existence.

POC stands for the point of creation of the thoughts, feelings, and emotions immediately preceding your decision to lock the energy in place.

Sometimes people say "POD and POC it," which is simply shorthand for the longer statement. When you "POD and POC" something, it is like pulling the bottom card out of a house of cards. The whole thing falls down.

All 9 stands for the nine different ways you have created this item as a limitation in your life. They are the layers of thoughts, feelings, emotions, and points of view that create the limitation as solid and real.

Shorts is the short version of a much longer series of questions that include: What's meaningful about this? What's meaningless about this? What's the punishment for this? What's the reward for this?

Boys stands for energetic structures called nucleated spheres. Basically these have to do with those areas of our life where we've tried to handle something continuously with no effect. There are at least thirteen different kinds of these spheres, which are collectively called "the boys." A nucleated sphere looks like the bubbles created when you blow in one of those kids' bubble pipes that has multiple chambers. It creates a huge mass of bubbles, and when you pop one bubble, the other bubbles fill in the space.

Beyonds are feelings or sensations that stop your heart, stop your breath, or stop your willingness to look at possibilities. Beyonds are what occur when you are in shock. We have lots of areas in our life where we freeze up. Anytime you freeze up, it's a beyond holding you captive. That's the difficulty with a beyond: it stops you from being present. The beyonds include everything that is beyond belief, reality, imagination, conception, perception, rationalization, forgiveness, as well as all the other beyonds. They are usually feelings and sensations, rarely emotions, and never thoughts.

CPSIA information can be obtained
at www.ICGtesting.com
Printed in the USA
LVOW09s2314210317
528034LV00031B/684/P